ELECTRONIC
MUSIC
PRODUCTION

THE BIGGEST MISTAKES &
TIPS AND TRICKS FOR
SUCCESSFUL
CLUB TRACKS

Copyright @ 2021, Limbic Bits Sound Design / Stefan Heinrichs
Translation: Philip Forristal
Electronic Music Production: The Biggest Mistakes & Tips and Tricks for Successful Club Tracks
Limbic Bits Publishing
www.limbicbits.com

ISBN: 9798505077832

On Motivation and Procrastination: Eleven (Bad) Reasons Why You Can't Finish Tracks 40

Sounddesign & Mixing Tricks 49

Electronic Music Production

INTRO: ABOUT THIS BOOK

Thank you for choosing this book. Before we dive right in, I'd like to say a few words about the structure of this book, how you can get the most out of it, and explain my motivation for writing it.

First of all: the individual chapters presented in this book are not written consecutively. You can easily jump back and forth between chapters and dive into the ones that fascinate you most. Nevertheless, I still recommend reading this book cover to cover and re-reading the most interesting chapters for you later on.

I've kept the chapters short, focus on actual tips on how to implement something straight away and avoid giving too much theoretical background information unless it is essential to understand the chapter. To get the most out of it, I recommend applying the tips straight away within the framework of an existing project.

The book is organized as follows: the first part deals with the basic requirements for electronic music production and includes a brief segment on the subject of studio acoustics. This is followed by our first major block: the biggest common mistakes you can make in music production. This part focuses heavily on mixing and arrangement and discusses several other fundamental issues. The following chapter 'On Motivation and Procrastination...'' describes how to optimize your workflow in the studio. The fourth major block in this book is focused on how to mix your most important sounds correctly and provides concrete instructions and suggestions on creative sound design.

In order to write a book that benefits as many readers as possible, I have to assume a basic level of knowledge in the field of music. This book will not explain how to program a simple kick loop. I will also not go into detail on specific sub-

you are buying a controller, be sure to check whether it already includes a DAW or sound generator, since hardware controllers are often packaged to include a stripped-down version of Ableton Live or Bitwig. Eight audio and eight MIDI tracks can already be sufficient even for more complex production projects, and if you do wish to upgrade, there are often discounts with bundled versions. Not counting the computer you likely own already, getting started with electronic music production can be done for under $250.

HARDWARE-BASED SETUPS

The roots of (modern) electronic music production lie in the realm of hardware devices. Producers would either synchronize drum machines, samplers and synthesizers with one another or control their machines by way of MIDI using a computer - at the time likely an Atari. Product names like the Roland TB-303, TR-909, TR-808 and co. have surpassed the confines of the electronic music scene and arrived in popular culture today: graphics featuring these legendary instruments have become lifestyle accessories and adorn t-shirts, shoes and bags.

Many purists still rely on hardware-based setups today. The heart of the setup is still the sequencer, or at least a MIDI clock, that synchronizes all the devices with one another. As ever, the talent of the musician is what plays the pivotal role for the quality of the final result. Extensive hardware setups are more a matter of passion and preference than necessity. I have heard masterful productions created on a minimal setup consisting of a computer, a DAW and a few plugins. With the appropriate apps, even a smartphone can be used to produce entire albums today.

For many musicians, producing with hardware is still preferable and more fun due to the immediacy it brings, and for certain sounds, hardware still has a distinct edge. A mix of both worlds is the most common nowadays, with many producers using a DAW like Ableton to control a selection of synthesizers and drum machines. Although I am of the opinion that you can recreate almost any genre-specific sound with most well-equipped synthesizers, there will always be devices better suited for certain tasks, like synthesizing bass, pads and so forth. I will give a few recommendations in a later chapter, but in this matter, it comes down to personal taste.

STUDIO ACOUSTICS

If you want to have an honest representation of your music, you will need an acoustically treated room in addition to a good pair of studio monitors. Your room will require more or less treatment in the form of absorbers and diffusors depending on its size and dimensions, ceiling height, and the materials used in the floor and walls. Studio acoustics is a broad and complex topic that can range from a quick calibration of your room to elaborate room-within-a-room designs and goes well beyond the scope of this book.

The good news is that bass traps and other absorbers can easily be built at home with a bit of effort and some good, old-fashioned craftsmanship. To dive deeper into the topic, there are plenty of great guides on the internet, for example: https://www.soundonsound.com/sound-advice/beginners-guide-acoustic-treatment

Studio acoustics seems like a very dry (pun intended) topic at first glance, and beginners tend to invest in sound generators rather than acoustic treatment when in doubt. But let me give you a bit of well-meant advice: before you invest in a bunch of sound toys, make sure that your studio monitors and acoustic treatment are up to scratch. On the internet you can find countless images of extensively equipped studios with thousands of euros of synths and drum machines.

Somewhere, hidden at the back of the production table, you may spot a meagre pair of speakers - often not even aligned with the listening position - that live a sad existence between bare walls.

Everyone should do what they enjoy most. But if you end up hearing only a part of what your synth battleships are capable of by setting the wrong priorities, you've missed the point. Especially for the reasonable assessment of the lower mid and bass range - ever-important to club music - electronic music producers should prioritize their choice of monitors and acoustic treatment. If budget or space constraints don't allow this, switching to a high-quality pair of (open) reference headphones is advisable. In this case, the material should still be regularly referenced on loudspeakers, e.g. in the car, on a smartphone or hi-fi system to avoid problems in the stereo image or bass range.

THE OPTIMAL PLACEMENT OF STUDIO MONITORS

Most smaller studios use so-called near-field monitors. As the name suggests, these speakers are designed for short listening distances of one to two and a half meters. In order for the sound to be transmitted in the best possible way, the listening position should be just behind the apex (from the listener's point of view) of an imaginary inverted triangle with three identical sides. The tweeters should be at ear-height, with the speakers pointing toward the apex of the triangle.

The path between you and the speakers should not be obstructed by objects, and the speakers should not be tilted up or down at an angle. If you have no other choice, you should avoid reflective surfaces in the direct path of the sound. Sound reflections can quickly cause phasing problems due to the difference in sound propagation times. This leads to certain frequencies being overemphasized, while others can be cancelled out completely.

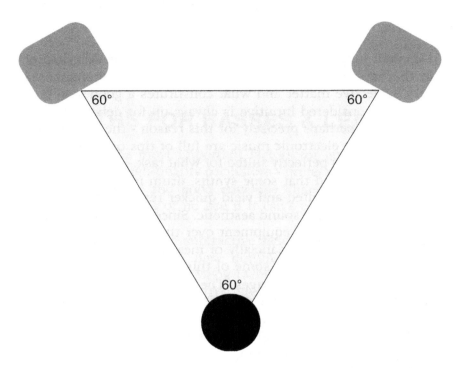

Image: Stereo triangle: the distance between the speakers and the listener should be identical. The tweeters should be located roughly at ear level.

SOFTWARE SYNTHS FOR BASSES & LEADS

In the software field, the U-He RePro 1 is a clear recommendation for analog sound. The Sequential Circuits Pro One emulation's incredible low end power puts many analog devices to shame. For Moog-type emulations, Softube's Model 72 and Arturia's Mini V really deliver. Classic Roland emulation is available from TAL U-NO-LX or directly through Rolands SH-VSTi series.

FM SYNTHS

FM synths are perfect for aggressive and organic basses. Some users will be initially suspicious of FM synthesis, as it is more difficult to grasp in comparison to subtractive synthesis at first glance. But once you have mastered the basics, the sounds almost program themselves. For beginners interested in FM, I recommend using an FM synthesizer with four operators followed by a filter in the signal chain. This way, the possibilities are not so overwhelming as to get lost, but you still retain the flexibility required for creative sound design. The filter functionality will be recognizable from subtractive synthesis, making your first steps easier thanks to quicker successes.

A flexible hardware FM candidate is Elektron's Digitone. On the software side, Ableton's in-house Operator is a great option. The freeware Dexed (https://asb2m10.github.io/dexed/) is perfect for more complex sound experiments. Not only is it free, but it also features the ability to import DX7 sounds and opens up thousands of (free) sounds to experiment with. But to be honest, the time spent listening through presets is better applied studying FM synthesis and will elevate your proficiency at FM that much quicker.

SYNTHS FOR PADS

To program pads, your polyphonic synthesizer should have at least four voices. This way, more complex harmonies and chords are possible. Extensive modulation possibilities are only important, if you're trying to achieve complex sound manipulation in your pads. To make your pad synth more versatile, the ability to play all voices simultaneously (unison) is a good add-on. This way, your pad synth will also handle basses and leads nicely.

HARDWARE SYNTHS FOR PADS

The synthesizer boom of the last few years has flooded the market with good hardware synths. Based on the basic requirements discussed previously, I can recommend the following synths without hesitation: The digital-analog hybrid Novation Peak, Oberheim's analog Matrix 1000, which almost approaches a polyphonic modular system due to its deep modulation capabilities (editor required), Korg's Minilogue XD, Clavia's Nord Lead, Roland's SH-01a and Behringer's Deepmind series. There are dozens more, but these models are all still in production - apart from the Matrix - and also all available at a good price second-hand.

SOFTWARE SYNTHS FOR PADS

The software world also features a lot of great synths for pads, so I'll just list out a few recommendations here. If you're looking to emulate analog synths, Repro-5 by U-He is a good candidate. Omnisphere 2 by Spectrasonics is an absolute industry standard for pads, but doesn't come cheap at $350. Considering the countless modulation and synthesis options, plus the countless samples it offers, the price is quickly put in perspective. Ultimately, it is suitable for almost all conceivable scenarios, with its main strengths in the fields of pads, basses and arpeggio leads.

In recent years, another company has shaken up the software market considerably: Output offers a wide range of VSTis, which are often based on a sample mixture of electronic and acoustic instruments. This results in a distinctly organic sound, perfectly suited to electronic music genre thanks to sophisticated modulation functionality. In contrast to the trance and goa staple Sylenth1 or NI's Komplete bundle, their presets also have not yet been beaten to death.

My freeware tip is the slightly geriatric Synth1 by Ichiro Toda (https://www.kvraudio.com/product/synth1-by-ichiro-toda). This VSTi was modelled after Clavia's Nord Lead series and still sounds excellent, especially for lead and pad sounds, despite its intimidating GUI.

SYNTHS FOR EXPERIMENTAL SOUNDS

An extensive modulation matrix, varied forms of synthesis, flexible oscillators, ring modulation, noise, multimode filters: if a synthesizer offers most of these features, you can be sure it's well suited for experimental sounds. If it's also modular or semi-modular, then the world of experimental sound exploration is your oyster.

HARDWARE SYNTHS FOR EXPERIMENTAL SOUNDS

In the realm of hardware, a great selection of synths has entered the fray in recent years. Recommended are the raw and growling Korg MS-20, Novation Peak, Waldorf Iridium, Elektron Analog Four with its flexible step sequencer or Clavia Nord Modular, which emulates a full-blown modular system.

For experimental sounds, an analog/digital eurorack modular system is also a great option. But be forewarned: as exciting as the limitless possibilities it offers may be, such a system can very quickly become a time and money pit.

SOFTWARE SYNTHS FOR EXPERIMENTAL SOUNDS

There are countless synthesizers available that are well suited for experimental sounds in the software field. The basic requirements mirror those of hardware systems: an extensive modulation matrix, as many modifiable parameters as possible and a strong sound are the most important requirements for the plugin. Due to the large selection and comparatively low prices, I'll take a different approach here and shortlist synths that are characterized by flexible synthesis types that are rarely - or only very expensively - found in hardware.

Modular synths as well as wavetable and granular synthesis are particularly exciting here. NI's virtual modular system Reaktor, U-He's Zebra, the Buchla synthesis emulator Madrona Labs Aalto, as well as the granular battleship Quanta by Audio Damage are great options. Ableton Suite users have access to the Max4Live Granulator device, which is especially powerful for experimental sound design.

Arturia provides a great hybrid solution with the versatile wavetable synth Pigments, which also features excellent filters for subtractive processing. Due to its highly flexible architecture, it's an excellent tool for FX sounds, complex pads and textures, but also for basses and lead sounds. Although Pigments is a fantastic allrounder, everything comes at a price, and Pigments is a true resource hog for your computer.

DRUM MACHINES & SAMPLERS

Hardware devices should provide individual outputs, step sequencing and enough parameters for sound design. On the one hand, this helps to shape your sound in the live environment, on the other, step sequencers are great for idea generation in the studio. The Roland TR series still dominates electronic music with its characteristic sound. Whether you are a fan or not - the fact is, these instruments simply work in the club environment. The well-equipped TR8S gets very close to this sound, and is a powerful, hands-on tool for playing live.

If you like to experiment, but also wish to fall back to the basic sound character of the TR series when you need to, Elektron's Analog Rytm is ideal. This hybrid of analog sound generation and sampling brings pressure in droves, but can also be used for experimental sounds thanks to its extensive parameterization options. And if that's still not versatile enough, you also have the possibility to import your own sample banks. Additionally, the MFB Tanzbär, Elektron Machinedrum (which is available for a good price second-hand) and the Akai Pro Force deserve a mention. All of these devices feature their own, characteristic approach and are well suited for electronic music.

SOFTWARE DRUM MACHINES

Emulations of the TR classics 606, 808, 909 are available in many variants. Examples include the Audiorealism drum machine, the D16 Nepheton, Wave Alchemy Revolution, and countless sample libraries.

Specialized software like D16 Punchbox, BazzISM or Sonic Academy Kick 2 deliver on kick drums. The advantage of Punchbox and Kick 2 are the layering possibilities inside the programs and droves of professional presets. The drum synthesizer BazzISM is a good way to go for very electronic sounds, while uTonic is a great tool to conjure up more unusual drums.

THE BIGGEST MISTAKES IN ELECTRONIC MUSIC PRODUCTION

BASS VS. KICK - WHEN THE LOW END IS A MUDDY MESS

The low end foundation is elementary in electronic music. To make your track really deliver in the club, you need to give this area on the frequency spectrum special attention. A common mistake is to pack too much sonic information into the low frequencies. Thankfully, it's easy to overcome this hurdle by making the necessary room in this section. To achieve this, you can use one of two strategies: 1. Making room with a clever arrangement or 2. Making room by organizing your frequencies.

In the first scenario, you simply place the kick and bass in their own individual space. If the kick is (mostly) placed on the one, you can place the bass on the 'and'. Like this: 1 (kick) - and (bass) - 2 (kick) - and (bass) - 3 (kick)... Make sure the instruments do not overlap due to long decay or release times. In such cases, you can either edit the volumes via the amp envelopes in your sound source, or you can use plugins to edit the volumes later in the signal chain (volume shapers). Alternatively, you can also manually draw volume automation directly in your DAW, which achieves the same result, but is quite cumbersome in comparison.

The second scenario usually occurs when kick and bass are playing at the same time, i.e. on top of each other. In this case, the frequency area occupied by these two components also overlaps. EQing is the simplest remedy: if, for example, the sub-bass covers the lowest frequencies in your track (from

25 Hz to 80 Hz), you can cut the lowest frequencies of your kick with an 18 dB high-pass filter with a cutoff at 75 Hz. If the low end contains frequencies under 25 Hz, you can safely remove these. These frequencies will not be audible later, but rob your track of volume in the mastering process.

Volume automation can also be a useful tool here. By lowering the volume of the bass whenever the kick triggers, you can make room for individual components in the mix. Additionally, there are other tools that help you achieve this goal quickly:

METHOD 1: SIDECHAIN COMPRESSION

Method 1 makes use of sidechain compression, which is very common in electronic music and will be encountered several times over the course of this book. To sidechain the bass channel, simply drag a compressor with sidechain functionality into it. Sidechaining enables you to compress the bass in relation to the volume of an external signal. Whenever the volume of the external signal exceeds a certain threshold, the compressor will trigger. In order for the presence of the bass to be lowered whenever the kick is playing, simply select the kick channel as the sidechain input for the bass compressor.

The attack time can be short, since you want to reduce the presence of the bass that is parallel to the kick. The release time should mirror the decay time of the kick drum. This way, the bass is ducked as long as the kick is clearly audible. In order to compress the bass by at least 6dB when the kick triggers, the threshold should be set to a low value. You can also set the ratio to a high value, 3.5:1 or higher is a good starting point.

One disadvantage of this method is that the compressor won't trigger at all in passages without the kick. To get around this, simply copy the kick channel and mute it. Then route the muted channel into the sidechain input of the compressor. To ensure that the bass is ducked for the duration of the track, program the muted kick channel to trigger throughout the track, even when the actual kick channel does not sound.

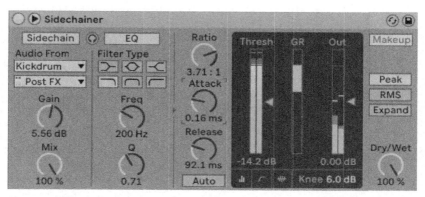

Image: Sidechain compression. Since the bass is compressed in relation to the kick, both signals will no longer negatively affect each other in the mix.

METHOD 2: USING TREMOLO EFFECTS AND PANNERS TO SHAPE THE VOLUME ENVELOPE

Method 2 makes use of a tremolo effect (or auto pan) to build a cheap volume shaper. The important thing here is that the effect features different LFO waveforms, including sawtooth, which can be synchronized to the rhythm of the track.

Note: if you use a different DAW, you can achieve this trick with the freeware Pecheng Tremolo. The plugin is available for free here as AU and VST: http://pechenegfx.blogspot.com/2014/11/the-plugin-pecheneg-tremolo.html

To make this work, I use Ableton Auto Pan, which is generally used to make sounds wander across the stereo image. First off, drag the plugin into your bass track. Set the amount to 100 percent to ensure that the entire signal will be affected by the Auto Pan. Next, bypass the stereo effect by setting the phase to 0°. Sine and triangle are suitable waveforms depending on which effect you prefer to shape the volume. Give it a try to see which you prefer. Now synchronize the envelope to the track tempo by clicking the small note symbol and set the rate to 1/4th. Finally, use the invert or offset settings to determine the starting point of the ducking effect and the duration until the signal reaches full volume.

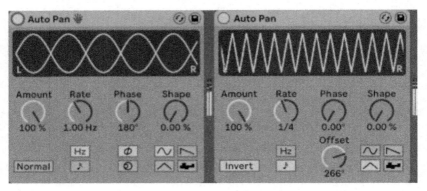

Image: Autopan plugins are a great and simply way to clear space in the mix (on the left: standard use as stereo panner, on the right: used as a ducking simulation)

ALL SOUNDS ARE DEAD CENTER

By creatively arranging the sounds in the stereo image, you can solve several problems at once: your mix will sound lighter, the frequencies aren't all stacked together and your overall mix will be more pleasant to listen to. Some electronic genres like psytrance deliberately use extreme panning to emphasize certain sounds and audibly move them through the stereo image.

Some instruments like kick and bass naturally belong in the center. For the majority of your sounds however, you have a lot of freedom when it comes to placing them in the stereo image. If you place an open hihat forty percent to the left, you should consider placing a counterpart - such as a shaker triggered in parallel or alternately - on the right side in your mix. Pads, textures and other atmospheres are well suited for processing with tools that widen the stereo image, so-called stereo enhancers. These tools use chorus, frequency-selective panning and/or different EQing for the left and right channels to widen the sound. Be sure to keep an eye one your stereo analyzer to avoid overdoing it: these tools are highly addictive, but can cause phase problems in the mix if used too liberally.

THE MIX SOUNDS CLUTTERED

Many mixes suffer from sounding too full or lacking defini-tion. Reducing the frequency spectrum of individual instru-ments to their most important frequency ranges can clean up your mix and make the overall track sound more tidy.

Don't hesitate to cut everything below 150-300 Hz - except for the kick and bass channels - with a high-pass filter. You won't diminish the auditory experience by cutting the bass frequencies of the pads, field recordings, or percussion. After all, this frequency range is already occupied by the kick & bass.

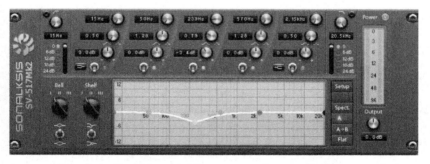

Image: Sonalksis SV-517MK2 EQ set to reducing the lower mids for a more transparent mix.

As a general rule of thumb, a lot of frequencies that muddy the waters are usually located in the 200-400 Hz range. Prob-lems might also occur above or below this range, but it's a solid point to start. Since you can't pull down the EQ on every instrument, it makes sense to start with the arrangement.

Piano-like sounds, strings, vocals, pads - these kinds of sounds quickly add up to an undefined knot you need to untie. Could the lead be played one octave higher to avoid conflicting with the pads? Do all the mid-heavy percussions have to play at the same time? It's better to make your individual elements shine by themselves, than to stir them all together into a frothy slush.

For overlapping elements, you can first cut the frequencies in the individual overlapping channels at 250-300 Hz with a wide band. Then sweep the band until the track as a whole starts to sound 'airier'.

The lower mids are often boosted to make a mix sound warmer. Boosting this frequency range also often leads to muddying the mix. Instead of boosting the lower mids, try reducing mids and highs. This way, you'll gain a warmer mix without the drawbacks.

THE MIX LACKS DEPTH

Your mixes will sound better immediately if you place your elements creatively in the stereo field and clean up unused frequencies. But it may still sound very two-dimensional. In this case, there's another possibility to tie the mix together and make it sound more homogenous: applying different depths to individual instruments and channels.

For this trick, we utilize the physical properties of sound. The further away a sound source is from us, the more energy high frequencies lose. You can easily reproduce this by cutting the treble for instruments or drums that you want to place further back in the spatial image. The effect is amplified by lowering the volume of the instrument.

With a reverb, you can further add to the spatial information of the channel. You can utilize the pre-delay, i.e. the point in time when the delay will be audible for the first time after the signal, and the reverb time to determine how far away the signal should be and how large the emulated room is. Try applying different reverb effects with different settings to your instruments. Give the snare a short and dry plate reverb, for pads I recommend trying a shimmer reverb to push it further back in the mix.

Reverb effects should be used with caution, as they can quickly clutter the mix. Always remember to use the equalizer to remove unnecessary frequencies. Alternatively, delays can be used to add depth to the audio signal. Delays won't clutter up the mix so badly and can be easier to handle.

MIXING WITH HEADPHONES

First of all, it is possible to achieve very good mixes with headphones only if you keep a few things in mind. However, it is important to always double-check your mix on other speakers: be it in another studio, in the car, on a smartphone or on a stereo system. This way, you can get rid of deficits that may not be apparent on headphones alone. In addition, you should be using high-quality studio headphones with a linear frequency response. If you plan to produce on headphones for long periods of time, you should purchase an open, ear-enclosing model. In the long run, these will be much more comfortable to wear. The good news: reasonably priced models from well-known brands like Beyerdynamic, Shure, AKG or Sennheiser are available from around $120 to $250.

Headphone mixes often tend to sound very flat. The mix lacks spatial depth, largely because space is perceived differently on headphones in comparison to regular speakers. On regular speakers, the signal reaches both ears with minimal time delay. Among other things, this causes our brain to generate a spatial sense of the audio. With headphones, this information is missing and the depth perception suffers. But if you are aware of this, you can counteract it by using various reverb effects, volume levels and panoramas.

Inexpensive headphones in particular tend to emphasize or mask the treble or bass range. When mixing on low treble models, you may compensate for these deficits using the EQ. If you then reference the track on another system, the hi-hats suddenly sound overly sharp because you were misled by your headphones. Professional studio headphones on the other hand have a very finely tuned frequency response. This is especially helpful for identifying noise in the mix and perfectly tuning the nuances in your channels. However, this level of detail also makes reverb effects stand out much more. As a result, you'll be using reverb too discreetly, which negatively impacts the depth of the mix.

The third big problem concerns the perception of the bass range, ever-important in electronic music. Headphones are unable to adequately reproduce (sub-)bass due to their small diaphragms. This leads producers to ignore the bass range, and results in overlooked problems in the low frequency range. The final mix often sounds boomy and unorganized in the low end, especially on large systems. Conversely, many consumer headphones emphasize the bass range to make their models sound fatter. In general, you should use consumer headphones only for the occasional double-check. If you rely on these models entirely when mixing, it is likely that you will perceive frequencies between 75 and 200 Hz as too loud, and consequently, these areas will be under-emphasized in the mix.

HIHATS AND CYMBALS ARE TOO SHARP

Hihats and percussion rich in overtones are an essential part of club music. But if they become too dominant, the resulting mix will sound cold and unpleasant.

An effective remedy against too dominant hihats is a de-esser. Originally intended for vocals, it can also be used to process hihats. A good starting point is 9-10 kHz: use the de-esser to soften sharp frequencies above this range. The nice thing about the de-esser is that it only activates when interfering frequencies exceed a certain volume threshold. Otherwise, the signal remains untouched.

If this still does not yield the desired result, you can bring out the heavy artillery and supplement the de-esser with an EQ. Many hihats and cymbals have a dull, metallic component at about 250 Hz. You can easily eliminate this by using a 24 dB high-pass filter at around 250-400 Hz. For the top end, use a high-shelf cut to lower the frequencies above a certain point. Start at about 13 kHz and move the starting point until you are happy. Proceed with this carefully: your overall mix could suffer if you cut too much.

MIXING WITHOUT CONTEXT

A popular mistake is processing individual sounds 'solo' until they sound the way you want them to. This is fine for passages where the sound occurs by itself. In combination with other sounds, this approach almost always leads to a muddy, overlapping mix. To avoid this, always listen to the respective channel solo and with the whole mix playing. Your focus must always be whether the sound works in the mix.

It is usually more effective to cut frequencies than to boost them. Since every sound should have its own place in the frequency range, you can safely do without frequencies that are not elementary to your sound. Approach the relevant frequencies from the top and the bottom with high- and or low-pass filters and cut superfluous frequencies, but be careful not to cut away your sound's character.

IGNORING THE PHASE

The individual channels are banging, but as a whole the mix seems thin and hollow? If the mix is clean and your arrangement is solid, you should check the phase of your channels.

When mixing signals that occupy a similar frequency range, phase problems can cause certain frequencies to disappear in the mix. This often happens when one signal is slightly delayed in relation to the other signal, as this will also cause the phases to shift slightly in relation to each other. In the worst case, opposing phases can cancel each other out, if the phase of signal A is shifted by 180° relative to the phase of signal B, leading to a complete cancellation of the signal. More likely, but just as annoying, this shift will diminish or amplify certain frequency ranges.

Phase problems occur when a signal in a similar frequency range to another is reproduced with a delay. This occurs often with:

- External instruments that aren't recorded with sample accuracy

- Plugins that do not feature automatic latency compensation

- EQs that are not phase linear

The solution: first of all, you should make sure that the latencies of your channels are automatically adjusted in your DAW. If that doesn't help, you'll have to do it manually. In most DAWs, individual channels can be dragged backward and forward in relation to the others with sample rate accuracy (or accurate to the millisecond). In Ableton, this feature is called 'track delay'.

Next, go through the channels and look for the culprit by muting individual channels and paying attention to changes in the mix. As soon as the mix sounds solid again, you have identified a problem candidate and can move on to the next step.

Now take the individual effects within the channel and switch them off and on one by one until you have found the effect responsible for the phase problems. If the effect offers different modes of use, you should select 'linear phase'. If you are using this effect multiple times in the mix, repeat this for all other instances to avoid further problems. If the plugin does not offer this function, it is usually best to replace it with another plugin.

If the cancelation occurs only at certain points within the track, individual audio clips are usually the culprit. As with the phase correction within channels, it is probably sufficient to move the clip minimally to the left or right. You may have to zoom into the clip to move it more accurately..

THE TRACK LACKS GROOVE

Depending on the genre, minimal shifts of individual notes (a hihat for example) can make a track sound faster and more driving (notes shifted forward by 1/64th) or more shuffling (notes shifted backward). Many DAWs also offer the possibility to apply existing groove patterns to your MIDI clips.

Claps and Snares can also benefit from breaking the rigid quantization to the 16th note grid. With practice, you can try playing your hihats and cymbals manually. If quantization is still necessary, it's a good idea to apply 70-80 percent instead of 100. This gives the track a more human feel and adds soul.

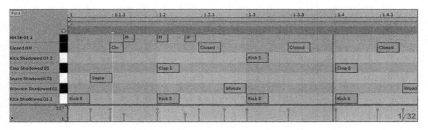

Image: Hihats moved slightly to the left will give the track more drive.

Loops recorded manually are a great way to support the groove. A good basis for this are specialized sample libraries. Either drag a suitable loop into your arrangement or cut passages from it to fit your track. By applying panning, playing some sections in reverse or applying some filtering, you can ensure the loop remains interesting and compelling over several bars.

YOU USED MEDIOCRE SOUNDS

First of all, I do not believe that there are bad sounds. You can always use your sonic material somewhere, both raw and processed. The important thing, as always, is the context and effort you put into shaping your sound. Surely you can get your thin kick to sit in the mix reasonably with layering, hours of processing and mixing the other channels around the kick. But this is not only highly inefficient, but also frustrating and a real killer for your workflow.

It's better to go for good sounds that work in your production. To stay with the example i just mentioned: especially in the realm of kick and bass, it's worth building a small stock of tried and tested sounds to recycle. By using them regularly, you will know their characteristics and the pitch of the instruments. This saves you time when mixing, because you get a head start on how to treat your sounds. Ideally, you've already checked your choice sounds for club suitability and know that the kick and bass will have a powerful effect on large systems.

By the way, there is also the flip side of 'sounds that are too good'. Many sample libraries have optimized their presets to such an extent, that a single sound greatly influences a broad frequency spectrum. In the mix, stacking these sounds will quickly produce problems if you don't counteract by EQing the individual channels.

BORING DRUM TRACKS THAT LACK ATTENTION TO DETAIL

Despite its repetitive character, electronic music lives precisely from subtle changes in the details. Nevertheless, many people do not pay the necessary attention to this when producing. Drum tracks suffer especially if they are limited to four-to-the-floor kick pattern programming with off-hihats, a clap on 2 and 4, and a cymbal every four bars, despite the many possibilities.

GHOST NOTES

Ghost notes are a great example. These are very quietly played repetitions between the main hits, traditionally used for the snare. But there's nothing to stop you from using ghost notes on hihats, percussion or even the kick.

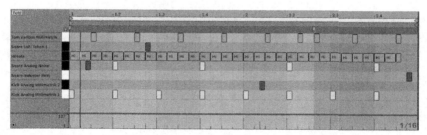

Image: Ghost notes (in dark grey here) are a great element to build a groove

Ghost notes should subtly support the groove (laid back or driving) in the background. If they are too noticeable, swap the sounds or lower the volume further.

HALF-TIME DRUM LOOPS

A good trick is to render a drum loop to audio and then pitch it down by twelve semitones at half speed to layer the main loop.

This can be done with most samplers by placing the audio file on C3 and then playing back the note from C2. With Ableton, you can also double the length of the loop and pitch down automatically by using the 'repitch' function of the warp engine (the warp engine in Ableton is a powerful sound design tool in itself when playing with its most extreme settings). Afterwards, cut the low end with an EQ. The lowering of the octave will change the frequency components of the sound. This layer is also perfect for effects like beat repeat or Izotope Stutter Edit, which would be too heavy if used on the main drum track.

DELAY AUTOMATION ON INDIVIDUAL DRUM NOTES

Another way of breaking up a rigid drum loop is to automate the effect send that contains the delay. This way, only single hits will be affected by the delay in contrast to the entire loop.

For the delay settings, I recommend straight or triplet repetition shifted backward or forward very slightly in relation to the tempo to build a groove. In addition, this may create interesting phase effects as the delay and the dry signal overlap.

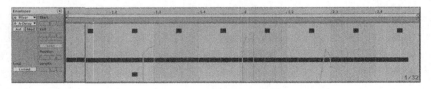

Image: Targeted delay sends on individual hits provide variety in the loop

This is a great trick to experiment and get truly wild results if you apply automation to the delay effect and vary its filter settings, feedback or delay time.

SLIGHT CHANGES IN SOUND CHARAC-
TERISTICS

Most sample libraries and presets respond to velocity (how hard you hit a key on a MIDI keyboard for example) by either playing different sample layers or changing the parameters of the sound. You can take advantage of this by assigning different velocity values to individual drum hits - the greater the span of velocity values, the stronger the variations in your groove.

For the kick drum you should use velocity variations sparingly - if at all. As a central component of the track, the variations should be kept at a minimum for this element.

Especially with hihats and percussion sounds, however, you can go the extra mile here. It is worthwhile to play with effect plugins later in the signal chain or fiddle with the synthesis section of your (drum) sampler. Using automation, you can assign different values for decay or release, change the filter cutoff or change the filter characteristics altogether. This may seem like a lot of work, but it will definitely pay off.

You can save some time by using slowly oscillating LFOs to subtly affect individual instrument parameters. A discreet flanger can also add a lot of value to the hihat group. The possibilities are endless - you'll just have to try it out.

THE ARRANGEMENT DOESN'T WORK IN THE CLUB

There it is: the perfectly mixed track. Nine minutes long, packed with chord progressions, complex rhythms and a three minute break sure to give you goosebumps. Then you finally try it in the club. Even though it's just the intro, the first dancers are already looking at their smartphones and by the middle of the break, the sad rest has also been swept off the dance floor. Only a few of the druggy crowd are still meandering around, drawing strange patterns in the air with their arms to your music. How could it have gone so wrong? The track was a banger in the studio, wasn't it?

Actually, there might be more than one explanation here: 1. The DJ screwed up and played the track at the wrong time or at the wrong place. Maybe this track is meant for sunrise at an open air, instead of prime time at the club. 2. You made a few mistakes in production that added up to catastrophe. There is the long break for one, which may just have lacked a few rhythmic elements as an 'anchor' for the dancers. Maybe the eclectic groove demanded too much of the crowd. Maybe there was simply too little or too much variety. There's no secret recipe that guarantees your track will be a hit in the club.

But you can gain valuable clues by using reference tracks. As a rule, you'll likely be able to assign a genre to your track. If it fits the attribute melodic techno, for example, you could simply go through the Beatport top 20 of the past months within this genre to ascertain what these tracks have in common and how yours differs from them.

FORGETTING TO FINETUNE

Melodies, bass sounds and pads can be tuned quite easily by ear or note input. In everyday production, however, it's easy to forget that kick drum, percussion and cymbals almost always have a fundamental as well. If, for example, the kick is a semitone above the bass, this will inevitably lead to a perceived disharmony. The track will have an uneasy note and the mix will suffer.

For your kick and percussive elements, the pitch will often progress from a higher to a lower tone in the space of only milliseconds - even for recorded acoustic instruments. This is quite intentional, as it gives the sounds more punch and character. But determining the fundamental of these sounds is often difficult due to the quick pitch shifting on the one hand,

and the nature of the sounds on the other: the kick is usually pitched so low that it is no longer possible to easily hear its note.

TUNING BY EAR

A simple trick will help you here, which I will demonstrate using the kick drum as an example. First, you determine the root note of your track. Most of the time, you will already know it, since you have recorded melodies that harmonize with the track. In this case, you can simply check the key of your track in the piano roll. Theoretically, you could now use one of your existing lead or pad tracks to play the root note repeatedly and tune the kick to harmonize with this note. Often, it is more practical to create a new channel to tune your percussion. Drag a synth into it that plays the root note with a simple, unmodulated triangle wave.

Then load the kick into a sampler and play it one octave higher. In this octave, find the corresponding pitch of the kick on your keyboard that matches the root note played by the triangle wave. A low pass filter may help you focus by clipping the unnecessary higher frequencies. You'll know you've hit the sweet spot when a slight flanging or chorus effect occurs as both instruments (kick & triangle oscillator) play at the same time. Fine tune the pitch of the kick until this effect is minimized.

Now lower the kick by twelve semitones (one octave) to return it close to its starting point. Alternatively, you can use the tuning control on your drum synth or sampler until you hit the root note of your track.

For hihats and other high pitched sounds, you can approach the pitch in reverse order. Here, you look for the root note of your track by slowly pulling down the tuning of the hihats until their frequency matches the tuning of the track. If you end up having to lower the pitch by a lot - say ten semitones - it's a good idea to raise the pitch by two semitones instead. This way, you'll still hit the root note of the track, but you won't have to make your hihat sound artificial to achieve true pitch.

Tuning should become an integral part of your production process and should be applied to all elements of your track. Every new element added should be tuned immediately to prevent problems later on. You will quickly notice your mix benefit enormously from proper tuning.

I HAVE DIFFICULTIES RECOGNIZING PITCH BY EAR - WHAT ALTERNATIVES ARE THERE?

Sometimes it can be difficult to tune instruments by ear - despite these tricks. It can also take several years to train your ears to recognize harmonies and correct tuning. Fortunately, there are remedies if you have difficulties.

One option is to use a tuning plugin. These are actually meant to help you tune external instruments like guitars. But you can also use them to help you tune your elements. Drag the plugin into the channel you wish to tune. To ensure a clean result, there should be no other effects in the signal chain between the sound source and the tuning plugin.

As soon as you hit play on the kick, percussion, etc., the tuning plugin should display the pitch. There is a catch, though: very short drum sounds are only displayed very briefly, and sometimes the plugin will not show any value at all. If this occurs, you can increase the duration of the sound with a longer decay and release or with the help of time stretching until the tuner outputs meaningful values.

EQs and analyzers are another alternative for displaying the note values of the frequency spectrum. Since notes are always assigned to a specific frequency, you could also use a frequency note table to achieve this manually, but this is much more time consuming.

Since the kick sits in the lower mids and basses, take a look at this range for information about the kick's root note. In the frequency curve, this value is located at the first dominant point, in our example at the note G2. If you adjust the tuning control of the kick, you can watch the frequency peak shift. With visual support, it is easier to gradually bring the tuning of the kick closer to the root note of the track.

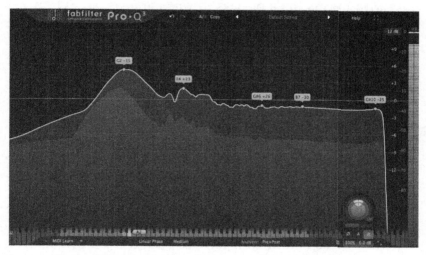

Image: Some EQs can display the notes of dominant frequencies

NOT EQ-ING THE EFFECTS CHANNELS

Using equalizers in the effects channels is an easy way to make your mix more transparent. Drag an EQ plugin of your choice in front of the reverb or delay in your effects channels. The plugin doesn't have to have any fancy capabilities - low and high cut will suffice. The point here is to prevent unnecessary frequencies from passing through to the effects in the first place. This will clear up your mix by ensuring that unwanted frequencies aren't amplified and multiplied.

It's a good idea to add a steeply sloping low cut at 250 - 350 Hz. You should be more careful with the high frequencies: combined with a reverb, these highs can give your mix extra transparency.

Caution! Many plugins add new frequency components to the incoming signal by processing it. Be careful that the outgoing signal from your reverb doesn't suddenly clutter up your mix with lowers mids or bass. If this happens, an EQ further down the signal chain will help with this problem. Alternatively, many plugins offer a built-in EQ for this purpose.

THE TRACK IS COMPRESSED TO DEATH

If you're using a compressor on every track, your limiter is working overtime and your analysis files are a solid black bar, then you've gone a bit too far on the compression.

To stand up to other tracks on Spotify, YouTube or in the club, your track has to be loud, there's no question about it. But that doesn't mean you have to sacrifice the dynamics in your track completely. Listen to your gut! If it tells you that your track is annoying after listening to it for a while, you should rethink your compression approach. The best remedy here is to use less of a good thing. To achieve loudness without losing dynamics, I recommend using parallel compression.

Parallel compression is often used on drum groups, but in principle it can also be used on the sum. How does it work? The basic idea behind it is to massively compress the audio in a first step and make it louder that way.

To achieve this, we need fast attack times and moderate to slow release times. You can use a generous ratio, say 4:1 to 8:1. Finally, lower the threshold so that the audio is compressed by -10 to -15 dB. If we leave it at that, however, we are back where we started: the transients are obscured, the track has an unpleasant thump and feels exhausting to listen to.

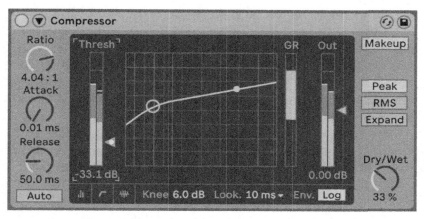

Image: Parallel compression (Ableton Compressor)

The trick with parallel compression is to mix the heavily compressed signal proportionally with the summed signal. Many software compressors offer a convenient solution for this with the dry/wet control. Increase the compressed portion slowly by raising the wet control. The point that still offers audible transients while making the track more present overall will be your sweet spot.

If you don't have a compressor with a dry/wet control, you can alternatively send your tracks through an effects bus containing the compressor plugin. By using send amount of your tracks and volume control of your effects channel it's easy to achieve parallel compression this way. Latencies should be accounted for, but most DAWs with latency compensation are able to do this by default.

NOT USING THE ANALYZER

An analyzer is a useful tool to visualize problematic and superfluous frequencies. Try working with the FFT-Analyzer Span by Voxengo (https://www.voxengo.com/product/span) - it's free and offers a great starting point.

The analyzer will show you issues in the low frequency range, for example, which your monitors may not be able to reproduce. Likewise, sounds that are too dominant quickly become noticeable as outliers on the curve.

Tip: you can combine an analyzer and an EQ to find problematic frequencies in individual instruments. Select an EQ of your choice that enables you to choose a custom bandwidth (also called "Q").

Set "Q" to a very narrow setting and increase the volume of the EQ band. By slowly sweeping from left to right, you'll be able to focus in on problem frequencies as soon as an unpleasant "whistling" or "ringing" is audible. Now you can lower the band until the frequency no longer interferes with the mix. It is a good idea to increase the bandwidth again to lower neighbouring frequencies somewhat as well.

THE MIX SOUNDS TOO DIGITAL

Many current home studio productions have a digital character. The highs are too harsh, the individual sounds too sterile, the overall impression is too clinically perfect. In contrast, analog productions are said to be warm, lively, and offer more depth.

But this isn't rocket science: the treble range of purely analog productions naturally sounds softer. Barely perceptible amounts of dirt, noise and small imperfections stemming from the integrated hardware sound generators, the mixing console, processors and effects add up audibly in the background.

Fortunately, simulating this digitally is relatively easy thanks to a great variety of tools that are available. Silky treble instead of harsh peaks can be achieved with saturation, for example. Analog tubes (though this behaviour may also occur in transistor circuits) add new harmonics to the input signal when you overdrive them slightly. The resulting sound is often described to have more presence and shine.

Image: Tape emulations are good tools to simulate analog sound (left Softube Tape, right Waves J37)

In the plugin realm, you should look at tube simulations, distortion and soft clippers for subtle use. The most important factor is how much you drive the saturation. Most plugins offer input, drive and gain controls for this. If your plugin does not, you can always raise the volume of the audio file or synth before it is fed into the saturation plugin. From the vast array of plugins in this area, I recommend Soundtoys Decapitator as a plugin "for all things distortion", as well as the excellent freeware Saturation Knob by Softube (https://www.softube.com/index.php?id=satknob).

Tape saturation as occurs in old tape machines is also a very good tool for making the sound feel warmer, especially since most plugins emulate several behaviours of these machines at once. Modulating settings such as drift, tape speed, wow and flutter (how much the tape "wobbles") will make the sound more lively and give you just the right amount of inaccuracy and imperfection.

To ensure the saturation gels with the mix, you should load your saturation plugin into a group or effect channel and apply it to several channels simultaneously. This allows you to set the saturation level for the individual channels more quickly, distort only individual frequency ranges with an EQ in the signal chain, and compress the signal evenly across several instruments with a compressor placed subsequently in the effect channel. Using the "solo" function of the effect bus, you can also better judge the harmonics added by the saturation.

You can easily add subtle noise and background atmospheres by making a few field recordings with your smartphone or microphone in a quiet environment and adding them into your mix at the end. This might also relax your attitude toward noise from external equipment. Don't forget: analog synthesizers aren't noisy, they breathe.

NOT ENOUGH ORIGINALITY...

"How does Villalobos make his kicks?", "what equipment do I need to sound like Bodzin?" etc. Occasionally, you stumble across these kinds of questions and the web provides a wealth of answers. For the learning process, it can be a good idea to rebuild certain sounds or even entire tracks. However, this approach should be limited to the learning experience. It should not be your goal to sound exactly like Bodzin and co. because there is already someone doing it that will certainly always be better at it. It is more important to use the knowledge you have acquired to develop your own, original style.

...AND TOO MUCH ORIGINALITY

First of all, if you don't have any ambitions for your tracks to be played in the club or you do not wish to perform for an audience, there are no rules. In the end, the only person who has to like it is you. Luckily, there still are enough clubs that leave a lot of room for experimentation. But in most other cases in electronic music - as in many other musical genres - the audience has an expectation you should not deviate from too radically.

Tracks should meet a minimum of conventionality so as not to overwhelm the audience for several hours and sweep the dance floor. Break the rules when it makes sense to deliver something compellingly original, but also use established structures to avoid making your life too difficult. A guiding principle might be: experiment with sounds, but be conservative with your arrangement. Reference tracks offer a good guideline.

NOT USING REFERENCE TRACKS

Reference tracks are indispensable as a basis for your production. On the one hand, there is the mix: if the track ranks highly in the relevant charts, you can assume it is played and works well in the club. The kick sits in the right spot, the bass is powerful and the hihats don't get annoying. Drag your favourite tracks into the arrangement view and try to understand and recreate the mix (not the melodies). Besides your ears, a good analyzer will help with this and provide information on the distribution of frequencies and volumes and the positioning of sounds in the stereo panorama.

In addition, reference tracks help you arrange and flesh out your ideas. While the creative process is fun in Ableton Live's performance view, turning your ideas into a 6-8 minute track in the arrangement view is often the tedious part. Again, reference tracks can serve as a useful starting point here.

To do this, take your individual clips (kick drum, leads, pads, etc.) and transfer them to the arrangement view of your DAW. Another audio channel is reserved for the reference track. Zoom into the track far enough to clearly See the waveform. Now you can use the reference track as a template: where does the kick come in, where does the break start and how long is it, how does the track continue after the break? Once you have roughly copied the structure, it will be much easier to work on the finer details. Now you've reached the point of incorporating your own style and accents without deviating too much from the club standard.

NOT ENOUGH FOLLOW-THROUGH

In the beginning, you had a clear idea or an inspiring loop. Over the course of time, more and more elements were added, the track bloated further and further and in the end you completely lost what you were going for. Less is more, especially in electronic music. It is better to follow a clear line with a few elements from beginning to end than produce a massively overloaded track that is made up of three individual ones.

YOU DON'T REST YOUR EARS

Truism: the ears are without a doubt the most important tool in the studio. Nevertheless, we tend to ignore the signals our body sends us. This is especially prevalent when you are buried deep in your flow and even forget to eat or drink while producing.

As a rule, you should rest your ears at least for the same amount of hours they were exposed to noise. So if you've been producing for five hours, you shouldn't listen to (loud) music or be in a noisy environment for at least five hours afterwards. For the latter, I recommend always bringing high quality earplugs for protection, no matter what the reaction of other club-goers may be.

Ear fatigue is usually not immediately recognized. A clear sign is when you are constantly switching back and forth between A/B comparisons and hardly notice changes, or constantly pulling up the volume to hear the mix "more clearly". Impatience and general irritability are also clear signs that you need a break. Listen to the signs your body is sending you.

In addition to the ever-important breaks, I recommend rarely monitoring at high volumes. The level should be equivalent to normal conversational volume. Another advantage is that you don't fall into the trap of equating volume with good sound, because the bass is perceived more strongly.

ON MOTIVATION AND PROCRASTINATION: ELEVEN (BAD) REASONS WHY YOU CAN'T FINISH TRACKS

If you're churning out track after track and have no trouble coming up with ideas, you can skip this chapter. In this case, you're probably part of a productive minority, whose lives are very well structured.

If, on the other hand, you often have the feeling that you're just not getting anywhere, even though there are countless ideas waiting to be completed on your computer, I recommend reading the next few pages carefully. Maybe this is a calming factor: a lot of producers feel the way you do, and the solutions are surprisingly banal and easy to implement if you follow through on them.

1. "I DON'T HAVE THE RIGHT EQUIPMENT"

One of the biggest excuses and an enormous time sink is to blame it on your equipment. Here's just one example of quite a few: Stromae's mega hit "Alors on Danse" was created using only Propellerhead Reason and a USB controller. Various artists have produced entire albums using only an iPhone and a lot of live sets are based on groove boxes like the Akai Pro MPC or the Novation Circuit. Equipment is definitely not the limiting factor.

There is equipment that can speed up your workflow and may provide more fun due to its directness. But searching for the "right equipment" should not become an obsession. Many ambitious producers have ultimately failed because they spend more time in forums and second-hand market exchanges than really understanding the equipment they already have.

A reasonably up-to-date computer, a DAW and a good selection of plugins are completely sufficient to produce great tracks. Don't let anyone tell you otherwise!

2. YOU'RE CONSTANTLY STARTING NEW TRACKS

Maybe this sounds familiar: you have a lot of tracks on your hard drive, all of them almost, but not quite, finished. At the beginning of a new track there is often an inspiring sample, a melody that's captivated you or the perfect kick/bass pattern. In this phase you are quickly in the flow and the track almost produces itself. Congratulations: you've cleared the twenty percent hurdle!

Unfortunately, now the real work begins. Working out the first draft, adding more channels, arranging and mixing. That's the next seventy percent before you get to the final mix and mastering. And it's exactly at this stage that many people lose motivation, because it's mainly busywork. It's no use going to the next project without finishing the old one just because a new idea is beckoning. In the worst case, the workflow of not finishing will become a habit.

Two tips to break this cycle: 1. Periodically clean up your hard drive every two to three months and delete tracks you're sure you won't finish. Be courageous and honest with yourself. Your goal is to free yourself from excess weight and have four to five really good candidates, than twenty mediocre ones. Use colors to assign status progress to your project folders on your hard drive. Green stands for final tracks, green-orange for the last ten percent (mastering and final mix), orange is work-in-progress (arrangement etc.). Red is the color for pure idea projects that have not yet made it to the arrangement stage. Your projects will be better organized and you can see at a glance, what your ratio of ideas to finished projects looks like.

You should also avoid jumping back and forth between different tracks. This will divert your attention and you will lose the core idea of the track.

3. YOU DON'T KNOW YOUR TOOLS WELL ENOUGH

Many make the mistake of cluttering up their hard drive with countless plugins, constantly buying new hardware or just cycling through presets, always hoping the next one will finally bring the sound they need. This way you'll only get results by sheer luck, if at all.

It's better to purposefully enter into a transition period after every purchase, and intensively work with the new tool in your arsenal. Learn how the plugin or synth behaves in the mix, explore possible strengths and weaknesses, and remove it from the setup if it does not help you.

For sound generators, it can make sense to produce an entire track using only this device. Admittedly, this will be a bit difficult with a 303 clone, but with a broader range of functionality you can easily produce an entire track using only a single device. This way you will get to know your synth intimately and also hone your skills in sound design.

4. YOU'RE SCARED OF THE FINAL PRODUCT

Sound familiar? track titles contain phrases like "*Final_Mix_V1", "Final_Mix_V2" etc... While multiple versions are often requested for commissioned production, you should limit yourself to a maximum of two versions, one of which should cross the finish line at the end.

Similarly, MIDI tracks can lead to working on progressions, sounds or melodies over and over again, never really reaching that satisfactory stage. Analog synths without internal memory have a clear advantage here: you're forced to record progressions in real time. After that, the result is final and you're not tempted to fiddle with it over and over.

You should use this to your advantage: freeze plugin channels in your sequencer or bounce the audio directly onto your hard drive. You're depriving yourself of the ability to optimize the channel further, but you've also made a final decision and can move on to other parts of the track.

5. YOU CAN'T LET GO

Once your arrangement is in place, you should be rigorously purging your track. This is one of the most difficult processes, because it means you need to say goodbye to a part of your creative work. But it is also essential to bring out the idea of your track and goes hand in hand with the intention of clearly following an idea from beginning to end:

Do you really need that second melodic channel, or would it make more sense to focus on one melody and make it more interesting by focusing on meticulous sound design? Do all percussive elements need to kick in at once, or would gradually switching tracks on and off add more drama to the track? Is it really necessary to play all the notes of your pad chords? You may get better results by deleting the lowest note(s) and letting the bass take over that part instead. In addition to a clearer structure, your mix will become more airy as a result of this process.

6. YOUR INNER CLOCK IS OFF

Partying late on weekends, sleeping in and lacking motivation for half the week with the Monday jetlag? You spend your evenings in the studio and call it quits with the feeling that this time you'll break the Beatport top 20, but the next morning, you're disappointed: what have you done?

As with everything in life, your body also has an inner clock for music production. Some produce better in the evenings, others better in the mornings. Usually, it's the case that concentration and thus the ability to select good elements for good results is better in the morning than in the evening. So you might use the morning hours to mix the creative session from the night before or to guide the arrangement into a structure that works.

Regularly try to set aside at least an hour in the morning for producing. If need be, just set your alarm clock an hour earlier. In the evening, make sure you stop in time so that your inner clock doesn't get out of balance. After a few weeks, your internal clock will be ticking correctly and you will become more productive overall, especially since you can start your day with a good feeling; after all, you started it with something close to your heart that you can build on later.

7. YOU DON'T TAKE ENOUGH BREAKS

Make sure to take regular breaks when you're producing. Aside from recharging your batteries with time off, you'll also rest your ears. When you're in the flow, it's easy to lose track of time. But don't set an alarm for your breaks. Flow is a state that is desired in creative work and sometimes difficult to achieve.

As soon as you notice that you're going in circles while making music or that you're getting tired overall, give yourself a break. When you do, leave all digital media untouched. It's best to exercise, go for a walk or pursue an activity that a) has nothing to do with music and b) keeps you moving. Movement gets your circulation going again and you actively prevent tension that quickly develops when you're concentrating on your screen or your equipment.

Taking breaks helps you objectively evaluate mixes, arrangements and melodies. After several hours of producing, you should let your track rest for a while and return to it the next day or - if the deadline allows it - after a few days freshly rested.

8. YOU BECOME DISTRACTED EASILY

Focus, concentration and flow - when producing, your ming should not be elsewhere. Turn off the Internet completely, close all programs you don't need to make music, and devices like smartphones and TVs have no place in the studio anyway. Use the full-screen mode of your DAW to avoid the temptation of going online while your next session is loading.

If you live in a noisy environment, it can be helpful to start your session with closed headphones. While you shouldn't rely solely on your headphones when mixing, they do a great job of blocking out extraneous noise and distraction for the first few minutes. You'll probably also get into a focused and relaxed state more quickly by blocking out external influences. After a while, you can easily switch from headphones to studio monitors.

9. FACEBOOK ETC. - YOU ARE STILL DISTRACTED

Social Media can be helpful for self-promotion, staying in touch with long-distance friends and to quickly find out about new trends. However, Facebook, Instagram, etc. are also a wonderful means to waste one's precious time and breed unhappiness. They rely on perfidious mechanisms to make the user depend on them. Bright red status updates during interactions directly target dopamine release - part of our brain's reward apparatus and ultimately one reason for the development of addictive patterns.

Admittedly, it's difficult to self-promote properly without the use of social media. I recommend setting aside one hour per week for marketing. Upload your tracks to the relevant portals and post news on your social profiles. I recommend you use two or three platforms regularly (e.g. Mixcloud, Instagram, Youtube) instead of having a half-baked presence everywhere.

A well-structured editorial plan for your posts will help you analyze what works and prevent pointless spontaneous posts about what you had for lunch. Pre-plan your week as much as possible and set a specific time in the day to respond to requests or comments. Follow through on this and leave the apps unopened until the next day when you are through. Otherwise, you'll quickly find yourself constantly checking your smartphone for updates, which will have a massive impact on your productivity.

10. YOU LACK ROUTINE

Devise a routine! By doing certain things over and over again in similar patterns, they become an integral part of your daily life.

In terms of your studio work, it can help to establish a routine that you reel off as you begin your sessions. This could be preparing a drink, five intentional minutes of fresh air, or a moment with an e-learning program of your choice. The latter has the added benefit of expanding your skillset. Music learning apps like Melodics or Yousician playfully help improve your timing when recording and teach you music theory or how to read notes. These are all things that will help you make significant progress in your production. Plus, after a few minutes, your brain will be tuned into making music because your concentration has already been focused in the right direction during this practice time.

The power of routine is easily transferable to different topics in music production. A routine of "finishing the track" can be very powerful. Set yourself the goal of finishing tracks at certain intervals, regardless of whether you end up liking the result 100 percent or not. You won't like every product afterwards, but you'll internalize two things in the process: first, you'll have broken the cycle of constantly starting over without finishing old tracks. Second, you hold a final product in your virtual hands, which is incredibly meaningful for motivation. Over time, these routines will settle in and your results will get better and better.

11. YOU DON'T SET DEADLINES

Deadlines are commonplace in most jobs. Product X has to be finished by a certain time. You can use this source of stress in the working environment to your advantage to get things done in a certain timeframe. Split your track into stages, like creative idea, mixing, arrangement, final mixdown. Assign a specific deadline to each stage. An overall deadline for the track as a whole can give a framework for the individual deadlines.

If the pressure of the mere presence of deadlines is not enough, you should consider a "penalty" if you fail to meet them. Perhaps you can involve friends or your partner in this. Present them with the finished result by time "X", otherwise... "Y".

This method has three advantages: first, you are likely to be more focused in your production. Second, you can track your successes easily, adding to your motivation. And third, you get used to an efficient workflow when producing.

SOUNDDESIGN & MIXING TRICKS

The last major section of this book will dive into the details. We will take a closer look at mixing and arranging and discuss the structure of the most important sounds like kick, bass, snare, etc.

In addition, I'll go into some style-defining sounds and show you how to recreate them. We'll discover some exciting tools and sound design techniques geared at filling the void when your creativity seems to run dry.

FINDING IDEAL LEVELS FOR YOUR CHANNELS

MONITORING AT HIGH AND LOW VOLUMES

You should adjust the volume of your monitors every now and then while producing. This way, you can easily identify channels that are too loud or too quiet. If overtone-rich sounds such as leads, snares or hihats are mixed too loudly, they will stand out strongly when the track is playing at low volumes.

Listening at high volumes on the other hand will allow you to understand the track's club impact. If the bass or midrange are too washed out, or the kick is too far in the background, you will quickly notice this at high volumes. Listen at high volumes sparingly to avoid tiring out your ears.

FADING IN CHANNELS GRADUALLY

An easy way to find the ideal levels for individual channels is to slowly fade them in. By raising the volume of the individual channel bit by bit with the rest of the track running, you slowly approach the ideal level until it fits perfectly. With this approach, you won't fall into the trap of having too many dominant elements, since you're adjusting the volume to the context rather than the other way around.

IDEALLY MIXING
HIGH FREQUENCIES

To make a mix sound balanced, good high frequency management is essential. If the mix sounds too harsh, the ears will tire quickly. If the harmonics aren't present enough, the overall impression will be lifeless. In order to gain optimal results, you should always evaluate your mix with fresh ears. An analyzer helps you localize problem areas. But don't rely on visual aids too much. Listen first with the screen off or your eyes closed. Make notes, then repeat going through the mix with the help of the analyzer.

If you get the impression that a light fabric blanket is muffling the sound, you should raise the frequencies between 9.5 and 14 kHz very moderately. A suitable EQ for this is a shelf EQ, which opens up the treble band and boosts all areas above the cutoff frequency.

Synthesizer leads and melodies usually occur in the region of 3-5 kHz. If the melodies aren't cutting through the mix enough, you can give the instruments a boost by slightly raising this range.

If the mix seems top heavy and harsh in the treble area, try cutting the 4-8 kHz range. Alternatively, you can boost the lower frequencies slightly, which has the psychoacoustic effect of making the high frequencies appear more subtle.

As per usual, our motto for EQ usage is "less is more". Our ears will react more strongly to boosted frequencies, even if it's just by a few dB. I therefore always recommend lowering frequencies in the first step, rather than boosting them.

USING AUTOMATION

Automated parameter changes give the track more life. Be it cycling panoramas, filter changes or switching individual plug-in effects on and off. Automation keeps otherwise monotonous tracks exciting even over long periods of time, and you should be making extensive use of this tool. To save time, it's a good idea to use a mixture of manually recorded automation and existing automation curves from the DAW, although you can always adjust the latter later. However, when it comes to introducing a degree of randomness and groove, manual recording of value changes will usually get you there faster.

Manually recording automation is especially useful for sound design. Examples include opening and closing filters, manipulating the attack time of the synth envelope, or accelerating/decelerating the LFO rate. In the case of purely analog synths without MIDI capabilities, manual is the only option and you might need a few takes until it fits snugly in the track.

Preset automation curves do a good job for fade-ins and fade-outs, panning (sine wave) or linear mixing of reverb and delay effects at the end of a break. Just try it out for yourself.

Excursion on the particulars of volume automation: I just mentioned fade-ins and outs. You can do this with individual channels, but I would strongly advise against automating the track volume. Once set, you deprive yourself or the person who mixes/masters your track of the ability to pull the entire track up or down by a few dB. You could lower the entire automation curve to adjust the volume, but Ableton provides a much simpler solution with the Utility plugin. For other DAWs, there is Free G by Sonalksis, a free plugin that emulates a MasterFader (http://www.sonalksis.com/freeg.html).

Basically, this allows you to do exactly what you would've done with track volume automation: you're automating the plugin's volume control. In contrast to just controlling the track volume, you now have access to the volume automation, but leave the actual track volume untouched. This way, you can lower the individual channel by a few dB in the final mix without touching the automation.

HOW NOT TO GET LOST

If you can't produce the track completely in one day, you should set inspiration anchors for the next session. It can be incredibly difficult to continue where you left off when producing. Be it because the feeling of the track is no longer there, or because you simply can't remember what you were working on. There are several methods you can use to stay on track with your tracks.

Firstly: make a rough sketch of the arrangement. This way you'll have the structure of the track right in front of you the next time you open the project, and you'll also have completed a bit of the tedious work part. With the rough structure, there is so much work waiting to be completed when you open the track the next time that there will be several starting points for you.

Secondly: create a to-do list in your set. Some DAWs offer notepads or markers to record important points in writing. The items should be as specific as possible, such as "try a different compressor on the kick", "distribute hihats with pan", "parallel compression on the sum." If you don't have a virtual notepad in your DAW you can simply use the analog equivalent. Alternatively, you can use the clip titles to write notes and comments.

Thirdly: when using analog hardware, there are several points to consider. Temperature changes can influence the behaviour of complex analog systems from one day to the next. This is especially pronounced in modular systems, where several components from different manufacturers are combined together. Many modules, even digital ones, also lack internal memory.

As a result, there's no way around fine-tuning your oscillators, updating digital parameters and re-aligning your envelopes. It's a guarantee that you won't be able to recreate the sound of your last session exactly. Sometimes this can be an advantage, for example when detuning suddenly gives your track an exciting new feel. It's precisely because of these happy coincidences that modular systems can be a real asset. Nevertheless, it is essential that you record your audio right away and preserve the clip for the following session.

MORE ENERGY
WITH MINI TRANSITIONS

Especially in the club environment, it's important that your production remains interesting and generates energy over the course of several minutes. A suitable way to achieve this is by introducing mini transitions. In principle, this follows the same functionality as the big break in the middle section, but on the micro level. With mini transitions, you connect individual patterns and loops with one another, rather than disrupt the arrangement with stark changes as is the case in the main break.

One example is introducing a reverse cymbal or crash every 16 bars in the hihat group ending on the '1' of the next bar. Another possibility is to increase the dry/wet setting of an effect to 100 percent over the course of a bar via automation, and then abruptly return to 0 shortly before the end. This works especially well with reverbs or the feedback parameter in delay plugins.

Conversely, deliberate omission of elements can also create tension. Just leave out a hit or two in a four-to-the-floor beat. By not fulfilling the listener's expectation of the straight beat, you subconsciously create tension in the listener's mind, and release it by reintroducing the kick in the next bar.

You can also apply this trick to frequencies. Every now and then, apply a crass high-pass filter to the kick or even the entire track. The cut can start suddenly or gradually and is held until the next bar begins.

Short transitions have another advantage: they support the structure of the track by "gluing" the individually arranged elements together.

PERFECT BREAKS
WITH REVERSE REVERBS

Surely you've heard of this one before: toward the end of the break, a strongly reverberating sound slowly rises and builds, blending into the rest of the track harmoniously as the main beat is reintroduced. Often, there's a simple trick behind this that has been used in electronic music for a long time, especially on vocals and leads. Basically, its just a combination of the original sound, the same sound played in reverse, and a lot of reverb.

First, you select the signal you want to base your transition on. For our example, I will use a short vocal snippet, as this is the sort of base material that will make the effect very pronounced. Using the reverse function, you reverse the playback direction of the sample.

Now apply a reverb of your choice to the reversed sample. The longer the break should be, the longer the reverb time. This will later determine the duration of the attack phase in the break. If you wish, you can also edit more parameters, such as stereo width and frequency distribution. I recommend setting the effect percentage to 80 - 100 percent "wet".

Record the signal from beginning to end - including the full tail of the reverb! If you don't like the result, play with the reverb parameters until you get it right.

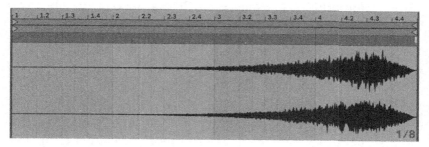

Image of the final audio clip: You can clearly see the reversed reverb building up slowly.

Once you are satisfied, simply reverse the recording. The sample will be played back in the original direction. The difference is, you have now introduced a reversed reverb that leads up to the sample, slowly building towards it.

You can also try this with delays. This very simple method is quickly implemented and also generally yields interesting results. Aside from using this technique in the break, you can also mix the reverb tail discreetly under the track as an atmosphere.

EDITING AMP ENVELOPES

You can further clean up your mix by tweaking the sound design of your individual instruments. Check if you can adjust the amp envelopes of your samples and synths and make them a bit more snappy by editing the decay and release times. This trick is especially useful for percussive sounds that transport their character even if they are played only for a few milliseconds. Go through all sounds with clearly perceptible pitch and reduce decay and release, making sure that the tonal character and the groove don't suffer in the process.

Then direct your attention to all hihats, cymbals, snares and claps and shorten them accordingly. If you are working directly with audio files, you can also use fade curves or volume automation. This may seem like a lot of work, but will pay dividends at the latest in the mixdown stage.

KICKS WITH PUNCH - HERE'S HOW

The kick drum is one of the most important elements in electronic music. I've already mentioned the all-important interplay between kick and bass earlier in this book. I want to go into more detail here and explain how to build powerful kick drums that won't have to shy away from comparison with other tracks in the club.

1. LAYERING

In electronic music, the kick is usually made up of several components: the low frequency part, a tonal midrange and a click right at the beginning of the sound. Many producers assemble their dream kick using different samples for each range. This Frankenstein kick can use the powerful boom of a sine wave oscillator, the midrange of an acoustic kick and a brief rimshot sample to round it off in the highs.

The trick is to layer the three samples on top of each other and using filters to have each occupy precisely the frequency spectrum it's supposed to fill with tonal information. Most drum samplers are capable of placing several samples on one note. Alternatively, you could play three clips simultaneously and resample the resulting signal. It's even easier to do this with specialized drum plugins like the D16 Punchbox (https://d16.pl/punchbox), Ableton drum racks or hardware devices like Elektron's Analog Rytm that combine analog sound generation and sampling.

In our fictitious example, the sine wave can stay as it is, because the overtones we would need to eliminate aren't produced by the deep sine wave in the first place. For the acoustic kick, we cut the low and high frequencies until the remaining mids no longer clash with our sine and our high end. Finally, we apply a high-pass filter to our rimshot that cuts out all frequencies except the range we need for our attack. The advantage of this not-so-simple method is that we gain total control over every aspect of our kick. This enables us to adjust one element irrespective of the others. We might want to distort only the mids or have more decay on the bass. With this approach, we can achieve that without influencing the other elements of our kick.

2. EQ AND COMPRESSOR

No matter if you use an existing preset or build your own via layering / synthesis: post-processing is essential in both cases, and you will almost always use an EQ and a compressor in the process. With the EQ, you will cut any remaining unwanted sonic information and set subtle accents, while the compressor is used to thicken the sound, define the attack phase and make the kick more voluminous.

Your compressor should be set to a long attack and a short release time. This way, the attack of the kick is not negatively affected by the compression and the kick will sound more powerful as a whole.

Depending on the electronic music genre, the kick might also be responsible for the bass portion. In this case, feel free to cut the low frequencies below 100 Hz in all channels except for the kick to make sure there is no conflict. To emphasize the bass portion of the kick, boost the frequencies around 40 - 80 Hz with an EQ. Ideally, you'll apply this boost in such a way as to bring out the root note more strongly.

Conversely, if you want the bass to take over the low end part of your track, you need to cut the kick's low end and boost the low frequencies in the bass channel with an EQ. Emphasize the kick at about 120 Hz with a narrow-banded peak. Lowering the frequencies between 200 and 350 Hz will also make the kick sound a bit more dry overall. Focus in on the target frequency by scanning the area slowly with a heavily boosted, narrow-banded EQ. As soon as the kick sound starts to ring and distort, you've found your target. Now you reverse the process by lowering the frequency slightly with a broader band.

Kick and bass should be mono below 150 Hz. This can be done very easily with plugins like Farbfilter Q3 or Ableton's utility tool.

3. SATURATION

At the end of the signal chain, you may also want to add some distortion. Used subtly, distortion will add additional overtones and give the kick more presence in the mix. In the techno genre, distortion is used quite liberally to make the kick more aggressive. There are different forms of achieving this, and whether you use distortion, overdrive or a tape saturation emulation is up to personal taste. The freeware plugin Saturation Knob by Softube is a great tool for this purpose. With just a few parameters and excellent sound, this plugin quickly yields results. https://www.softube.com/index.php?id=sat-knob

Rumor has it that some well-known producers like to "borrow" their kicks from other successful productions for their own tracks. Legally, this is probably no longer a grey area, but you can try this method for your own productions and try to recreate a kick if you like it.

CLAPS AND SNARES

At the very beginning, you should analyze your clap or snare and compare it with what you want to achieve. Is the sound fat or flat? How long is it audible? Is its core sound more metallic or more based on white noise? Does the sound work with my track, and what is it I actually want to achieve with it?

There are basically two approaches when you are designing the sound of your claps and snares (note: referred to only as "snare" in the following): either they are mixed subtly in the background with the objective of diversifying the sonic fabric of the loop, or they are placed powerfully in the foreground, as is often the case with harder sub-genres in electronic music.

The former can be quickly implemented by reducing the high end, lowering the volume and using a good amount of reverb to push the signal further back in the mix. If it's still too dominant, try softening the attack time with a transient designer or in the synthesis process to have the sound fade in slightly.

To have the snare work as a dominant element in the front of the track, the following procedure is recommended: as so often, we use the EQ to generously cut the bass range, at least from 60 Hz. I deliberately choose a low value here, since some flat-sounding snare drums benefit from a narrow-banded boost around 60-120 Hz to sound fuller. If the snare already sounds quite good in the low end, you can cut everything below 120 Hz with a high-pass filter (24-36 dB), ensuring that the kick and the snare don't conflict in the mix.

For most snare drums, the "warmth" is situated in the 120-250 Hz range. Depending on the needs of your track, you may want to boost this area. The 250-400 Hz range tends to clutter up the mix a little bit. You can lower this area with a broadband EQ by about 4-8 dB. To ensure that the snare is able to cut through the mix, you can boost the frequency spectrum between 2-3,5 kHz. To achieve a distinct whipping or slapping sound in the snare, you can boost between 6-8 kHz. Finally, you can add some shine and sparkle to the snare by boosting around 10 kHz.

The compressor settings are similar to those of the kick: middling attack values to allow the snare's attack to pass through, a ratio around 4:1 to 8:1, and longer release times to thicken the snares decay phase, ensuring the snare will sound fatter overall. You can amplify this effect by placing a reverb before the compressor.

If you want the snare to really pop off, you can also apply distortion to the snare and boost 1,5-4 kHz with a narrow-banded EQ.

HIGH PASS FOR VOLUMINOUS BASSES (...AND KICKS)

A high pass filter for fatter basses? What seems contradictory at first glance is a popular trick that has been converted to plugin form with Little Labs/UA Voice of God and its freeware counterpart Bark of Dog 2 (https://www.bozdigitallabs.com/product/bark-of-dog/).

This trick works by utilizing a resonant high pass filter to cut low frequencies while boosting the frequencies around the cutoff value. This makes the bass more transparent and gives it more punch at the same time. If you don't want to use a specialized plugin, you can also achieve this with most EQ and filter plugins. First, open a resonant high pass filter as an insert effect in your kick or bass channel with a slope of 24 or 36 dB. Now raise the resonance (Q) generously. Set the cutoff frequency somewhere between 35 and 120 Hz, depending on the root note of your kick or bass. In a last step, you can fine-tune the resonance until you find perfect balance.

If you're unsure how much to cut, it's better to let through less bass than too much to ensure less problems in the mix-down stage.

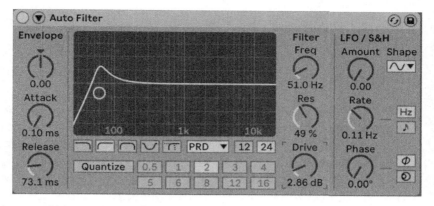

Image: Ableton Auto Filter

Tip: If your filter offers saturation controls (drive), you can add additional volume to the signal.

MORE TIPS FOR FAT LOWS

Next to our high pass trick, there are several other ways to fatten up your low end. Let's take a look at some of them.

METHOD 1 - DETUNING AND OCTAVES

If your synth has two oscillators, try slightly detuning them in relation to one another with the finetuning controls. For example, a finetuning value of +7 cent on one oscillator and -7 cent on another will produce a hovering feeling, and listeners will perceive the sound as much wider in the spectrum. More sparsely equipped synths simulate this effect with puls width modulation (PWM). By modulating the width of the square wave oscillator via LFO or envelope, PWM produces a similar acoustic effect to the detuning of two separate oscillators.

If you also tune the second oscillator 12 semitones lower, the overall effect will be somewhat more subtle. On the other hand, the second oscillator will also pack more punch in the low end...

METHOD 2 - UTILIZING SUB BASS

...which brings us right to our second method. Here, you layer the sound of your bass with a simple lead sound consisting of a simple sine or triangle wave. Both channels play the same melody, but the sine wave should be located one octave below your bass sound. In order for this to gel naturally, be sure that the volume envelopes in both channels mirror each other as far as possible.

METHOD 3 - EFFECTS

There are also a number of great effects ideally suited for fattening up your basses. The most obvious is the EQ. Boost the lows and lower the frequencies around 200-350 Hz to make sure your mix won't get too muddy.

A discreetly used chorus or reverb effect will broaden your sound a bit, but be sure these effects don't create too much clutter in the low frequency range. Some plugins feature crossover functionality, which allows you to have the effect apply only to a certain frequency range. If you don't have access to this function, you should incorporate an EQ or utility plugin into the effects chain to convert any frequencies below 120-150 Hz to a mono signal.

Use overdrive, bit crushers and distortion to add harmonics to your bass sound. This will make the bass sound more forward and aggressive. If the effect is too pronounced, consider adding a compressor after these effects to reel them in a bit.

ROLLING KICK DRUMS

In techno, you often have the feeling that the kick drum is somehow 'rolling'. Creating this effect is relatively simple. Often, it is simply a reverb sourced from the drum signal and integrated perfectly into the rhythm via sidechain compression.

First, you drag the following effect sequence into a channel that is set to receive the audio of the kick channel via send: EQ > reverb > another EQ for sound design > compressor with sidechain functionality.

With the first EQ, you cut the sub bass range and the treble of the kick. Be careful not to cut too much of the low end, as this signal is meant to constitute the off-bass to the kick. A value around 30-50 Hz with an 18 dB slope should be sufficient. For the treble, you can cut to your heart's desire. The clipped kick is now fed into the reverb.

The reverb will create the sonic basis for the rolling bass. Feel free to experiment, until you have found the perfect sound for you. A good starting point is a plate, room or echo algorithm set to a medium to large space with a generously set decay time. The effect amount should be set to 100 percent. You do not want any clear parts of the kick signal to be audible in the effects channel. Set the pre-delay to 0 and switch between echo, room and plate modes until you like what you are hearing. Another method is using high pre-delay values and short decay times to generate an off-bass. See what you can do with both approaches.

Our reverberated signal is now fed into the second EQ, which will take care of the sound design portion. A high cut at 150-300 Hz shapes the signal and pushes it more into sub bass territory. You can boost the bass between 50 and 90 Hz with a narrow band - ideally targeting the root note of the kick. Also apply a steep low cut at 20-25 Hz to get rid of any frequencies that are too low to be audible even in the club and will just cause problems in mix and master.

Sidechain compression applied at the end of the signal chain will help you merge the kick and the off-bass into a single, rolling unit. To do this, feed original kick signal into the sidechain input. Set the threshold to a low value to get a good pumping effect. The ratio should be set around 4:1, attack and release should be located in the lower range (1ms/50ms). If possible, use the lookahead functionality (1ms) so that the ducking will be perfectly timed.

GENERATING NEW DRUM SOUNDS WITH DELAYS

Irrespective of their use to support the groove, delays are also a great sound design tool. Basically, you want to create completely new sounds based on the incoming audio, rather than just repeating it. This may sound daunting at first, but it is really quite simple if your delay has an internal EQ or filter that can be applied to the delay signal. Alternatively, you can also use an external filter dropped later in the signal chain.

Let's go through the process with the example of a four-to-the-floor kick. First, you insert a delay plugin with an internal EQ into the channel housing your kick drum. I will be using Ableton's Echo delay for this. Set the dry/wet to 20-40 percent and the feedback to 40 percent. These values are flexible and are just mentioned for you to follow this example. The delay time determines when your second sound will be played in relation to the kick.

Next, we'll do the actual sound designing by emphasizing and cutting away certain frequency components. By setting a low cut at 700-800 Hz and a high cut at 3,5 kHz, we can transform the kick sound into percussion. If your delay's filter offers resonance, you can also emphasize the cutoff frequencies.

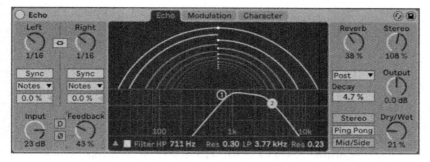

Image: Applied minimalism - delays with an internal EQ/filter section are great for generating interesting percussion sounds.

If you automate the values of both delay times ever so slightly, some frequencies will cancel each other out through opposing phases, similar to a flanger/phaser. This effect will intensify with higher feedback values. This can be especially powerful for producers with a minimal production philosophy: with comparatively few tracks and effects, these subtle changes keep your channels interesting.

DUB TECHNO CHORDS

Basic Channel, Rhythm & Sound, Deepchord and similar producers are known for a very special sound: dub techno. Besides noise and very deep, bass-heavy kicks, it's the metallic, psychedelic chord sounds that characterize this genre. In this chapter, you will learn how to make them.

We beginn with a relatively simple triad, which you can achieve through synthesis with three differently pitched oscillators (usually the root note plus 3, 7 semitones) or manually by actually playing the triad. A sawtooth rich in overtones is a great basis for this kind of sound. If your synthesizer is capable of outputting noise, you may already want to introduce some to go along with your chord at this point.

Set the amp and filter envelopes to hard attack and moderate decay and release times and dial in 30-50 percent sustain.

Higher attack times will push the sound further in the pad direction. The low pass filter in the synth is already cutting some of the harmonics. Dub chords rely on modulation, so use the LFO and the filter envelope to dial them back in. The more layers are modulating, the more interesting the end result will be. That's it on the level of sound generation, let's move on to the all-important effect sequence:

Synth > (Delay) > Band Pass Filter > Delay > Reverb > Phaser > Sidechain Compressor

Our first effect in the chain will be an analog sounding multimode filter that we set to band pass. I will be using Ableton's Auto Filter, but any band pass filter will do. Set the slope to 12 dB and add some resonance - this will later emphasize the metallic character of the sound. The filter frequency should focus on 350-500 Hz, but we will later modulate this with an LFO set to a moderate speed. You can also introduce an envelope follower to the filter frequency. As I said, the more modulation you add, the dubbier the sound will be.

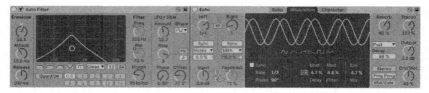

Image: Dub chords gain their sonic depth through an intricate effects chain with heavy modulation.

Next, the second essential element comes into play: a solid-sounding tape delay, ideally with the option of introducing a resonant filter. Fortunately, Ableton provides such a delay with Echo. By setting the delay mode to ping pong and choosing different times for left and right, the delay will generate a broad stereo sound. With Echo, you can amplify this effect via the stereo setting. For other delays, you can use external plug-ins to broaden the stereo panorama (one example is the freeware Stereotouch https://www.voxengo.com/product/stereotouch/). Choose a high feedback value, but not so high as to trigger self-oscillation. You can intentionally trigger this effect later in the track, preferably in combination with tempo changes to produce interesting, authentic breaks. In the arrangement, you can use automation to subtly change parameters like filter resonance or effect amount.

In the case of Echo, a reverb is already integrated into the plugin. If you are using a different delay, you should add in a reverb now. Choose a reverb with spring or plate characteristics, in other words, a metallic and more artificial sounding reverb. In the original dub, spring reverbs where a frequently used effect; almost every second snare hit is 'refined' with this fluttering sound. Select a generous effect amount and decay parameters. The tinny reverb character is essential to this sound - subtlety is not appropriate here.

As our penultimate component, we will set another sonic accent with a phaser. The parameters vary greatly depending on the application, so I won't give specific instructions here. A good starting point is a dry/wet setting of 25 percent and an accent on the mid-range frequencies with slight modulation by a slow to medium speed sine wave LFO.

Optional: to give our sound even more movement, insert another delay between the sound generator and the band pass filter. Play around with the delay times, try different modes (ping pong vs. stereo) and apply slight modulation to the speeds. The pitch should be changing slightly as you change the delay times, just as with the tape echo.

At the end of the signal chain, insert a sidechain compressor and let it pump more or less depending on your personal taste. If you are an Ableton user, you are welcome to download this Ableton rack instrument as a preset for free on my site www.limbic-bits.com.

WOBBLY PADS AND LEADS AKIN TO BOARDS OF CANADA, TYCHO AND OTHERS

An old cassette that has been played so often that the tape has wrapped itself around the sound heads many times has a truly distinct sound. These sounds have a special kind of charm that can be used in any genre. In this chapter, you will learn how to reproduce vintage tape effects.

The basis for this is a soft pad sound devoid of overtones: one or two slightly detuned oscillators (sawtooth/pulse), a low pass filter with 12 or 24 dB slope, some resonance and middling attack and release times. To make our sound even airier, generously cut the lows and lower mids with an EQ or high pass filter.

METHOD 1 - THE OSCILLATOR APPROACH

Now we add the necessary vintage character to the sound. We choose an LFO with sine or triangle wave and route it to the oscillator's pitch.

Image: A sine LFO that subtly automates the pitch with a bit of added noise provides a nice emulation of a vintage tape.

Some synthesizers, like Ableton's Analog which I am using in this example, offer a dedicated LFO for vibrato only, which makes it perfect for this kind of sound. For that extra bit of retro vibe, you can add some noise to this simple sound if your synth is equipped to do so.

METHOD 2 -
THE TAPE SIMULATION APPROACH

If your sound generator lacks LFO functionality or if you want to apply this effect to an audio sample, you can also achieve a similar result with specialized plugins that emulate tape recorders. The advantage here is, that these effects are expressly intended to emulate tape saturation and its behaviour, which means softer highs and a vintage feel overall.

For the lyre type effect, increase the wow & flutter parameters slowly until you reach a level that sounds good for you. Now modulate the 'rate' parameter to set the speed of the vibrato, and your sound is good to go.

Many tape emulations offer the possibility to switch between different tapes, tape age settings and degree of wear. To generalize, we could say that the older the emulated behaviour, the less overtones and the more noise you will have. And this is exactly what we want to achieve that vintage feeling.

A recommendation for owners of NI Reaktor 6: with the free "VHS Audio Degradation Suite" by James Peck, you'll gain a great VHS tape emulation with a lot of functionality. Everything needed for ageing sounds is included. The sound palette ranges from subtle tape saturation effects to massive deconstruction of the audio material, including distortion, noise, flutter and wow. Even the ground noise of some of these devices was incorporated in this piece of software.

THE POWER OF RANDOMIZATION
PART I - NEW INSPIRATION
FOR DRY SPELLS

Many software synths and sequencers offer a random function (sometimes called alternate) to create new sounds and melodies. You can also use this as inspiration at the push of a button. Ideally, you can also influence the degree of randomness, so different amounts of parameters are randomized depending on the field of application. Sometimes, randomness may only be introduced to certain areas of the synth, for example to the oscillators or the envelopes. If you want to keep the timing of the synths (LFOs and envelopes), but wish to modulate the sound heavily, you should randomize the oscillators and the filter.

The same applies to randomization in sequencers. The TB-303 emulation ABL Bassline allows you to randomize the entire sequence, or only the pitches associated with the steps. An 'Alter Pattern' mode rearranges all programmed notes, shifts and accents without changing the pitches of the notes themselves. This is very handy for quickly changing the vibe of your sequence without having to readjust all the pitches to match the root note of your track.

Random functionality can be found in many plugins, DAWs and Max4Live devices, and you should definitely give randomization a try.

THE POWER OF RANDOMIZATION
PART II - ANALOG CHAOS

This trick is great to fill sterile digital sounds with real, analog life. All you need is an LFO with S&H and key reset, as well as the option to route this function to the frequency (and, if possible, finetuning) of your oscillators. This will change the pitch minimally with each attack, mirroring a behaviour that was common in older analog synths.

Choose a slow frequency, otherwise you will quickly find yourself in the realm of blippy computer sounds from the Sci-Fi movies of the 70s. If your LFO offers one shot mode, you should have it activated. This way, the LFO will only trigger once per keystroke and the pitch will remain constant if notes are held for long periods of time.

We are aiming for a very subtle modulation here. +/- 10 cents should be a high enough value to modulate the finetuning setting. If the only setting you can route to is pitch, select +/- 1 (value, not notes!). If you have several oscillators, you should either modulate them independently, or only one at a time. The sound might become too static if we apply these modulations to all oscillators in sync. By activating reset, you ensure that the LFO restarts with every keystroke and does not switch back to the start of the curve in the first few milliseconds of your sound.

GOOD TOOLS FOR EXTRAORDINARY CHORD PROGRESSIONS

Diving into music theory can be a good approach to get started on more complex chord and melody progressions. Tonal electronic music benefits greatly from major/minor changes, the use of multiple scales or even the incorporation of microtonal scales from distant geographical regions.

However, many producers lack the theoretical knowledge or don't want to approach a track with pen and paper. Fortunately, there are simple tools that produce great chord ideas with minimal effort. I'll introduce some of them here.

For Ableton Suite users I recommend Schwarzonator 2.0, a Max4Live device that runs within the Ableton framework. It was developed by jazz/electronica producer Henrik Schwarz and is available here —> https://www.ableton.com/de/packs/schwarzonator/.

Equipped with only a few choice parameters, it quickly produces harmonically fitting chord progressions. As a bonus that's especially helpful for live performances, you can also program and save your own sets of chords.

Another comprehensive chord tool is Liquid Music by WaveDNA (https://www.wavedna.com). The plugin lets you draw or import your own melodies and creates exciting chord progressions on the basis of your melody.

Liquid Music is also a great starting point when ideas just won't present themselves. Just drop in a few notes and the program will generate several variations as a basis for further editing. But this amount of complexity has its price: the melody option will cost you about $200. This also includes Liquid Rhythm, a second M4L device specialized on rhythm generation.

If Liquid Music is too complex for your needs, Obelisk by FrozenPlain (https://frozenplain.com/product/obelisk/) is a slightly more limited MIDI-Plugin specialized on the generation of chord progressions. For $25, the intuitive software offers a good range of ready-made scales and progressions.

Captain Chords 2.0 is a bit more extensive and actually quite similar to WaveDNA. For about $80 you get a complete package including a chord generator, as well as different scales and rhythm variations that help you get out of your creative rut with ease. Find more info and a demo version here: https://mixedinkey.com/captain-plugins/captain-chords/

Many plugins also come with their very own chord progression templates. Some of the sample instruments featured in Native Instruments Kontakt offer a special section to select the root note, scale and chord type.

CREATING SOUNDS FROM YOUR OWN SAMPLES

Using your own sounds instead of off-the-shelf presets can greatly improve your production. Sampling your own synth-based sounds and incorporating field recordings - sampling external sound sources - offers infinite possibilities to create something completely new. This way, you just might create that missing and unique element that will make your track stand out.

The great thing here is that hardly any equipment is required. The most low-tech option is using the voice memo function of your smartphone, as that is what would always be readily available. But smartphones will only amplify external signals (without noise) to a certain extent. I recommend purchasing a special microphone for smartphones like the iQ6 by Zoom (iOS) or the SmartLav+ clip-on microphone by RØDE, priced at $50 and $110 respectively. If you want to go a step further, you can go for Zoom's H4n Pro or H5 without hesitation. These field recorders are equipped with good microphones, but also allow the use of high-quality microphones thanks to XLR inputs and phantom power. This allows accurate field recording with directional microphones.

A set including a directional microphone will not exceed $400 and guarantees maximum flexibility, and the field recorder by itself can be purchased second-hand for as little as $150. A nice side effect when you're out on a field recording trip: you'll discover a completely new world along the way. Every sound stands out and is perceived in stark contrast to how you would listen in everyday life. Wind rustling the leaves in the treetops, insects humming, even places with a lot of traffic or people (bus stops) appear in a completely new light and are great candidates for background atmospheres.

Although I tend not to bring electronic equipment on a holiday, I make an exception for the field recorder and always keep it close at hand. I've recorded the metro in Madrid, the gurgling breaking of waves on rocks, or the industrially repetitive sound of an out-of-order escalator as I was bored from waiting for a delayed connecting flight.

A field recorder is also an extremely useful tool in the studio, for example to quickly craft percussion sounds with everyday objects. Salt and pepper shakers are quickly converted to percussive shakers, and a metal salad bowl from Ikea can act as a low budget singing bowl. And that's just the beginning of your kitchen orchestra. Here, too, you will discover a completely new way of hearing the sounds your everyday objects make. Owning a field recorder will inevitably turn you into a sound researcher.

SAYING "YES!" TO EXTREMES

You want exciting sounds that no one has likely used before? Then you should turn your attention to the limits of sound. I'm talking about extreme pitches, massive time-stretching, heavy distortion and so forth.

For sound generators, I like to focus on how low the oscillator frequency goes and if the frequency can be decoupled from the note input. An extremely low sawtooth or pulse wave will sound like rhythmic clicks. This is possible with most modular systems, but some hardware synths (like the Novation Circuit and Peak) are also able to output extremely low frequencies.

Conversely, you could pull up the frequency of an LFO and route it to the audio output until the signal becomes audible. These clicks are a nice start, but the real fun begins wenn you modulate several slow oscillators or route them to other parameters of the sound generation process (Filter FM). Similar to a swinging Geiger counter, this will create granular clouds of sound made up of irregular clicks. You can also recreate this pitch-down process using samples.

For audio files and samples you can also use another trick for sound design: extreme time-stretching. With time-stretching, the idea is to change the playback speed of the sample without affecting the pitch. Normally, this functionality is used to adjust the sampled melody or beat to the speed of the track, which is often done automatically nowadays through warping. But time-stretching can also be a real treasure trove for interesting sounds.

Think of an audio file as a succession of individual sound slices that are cycled through one after the other over time. By massively reducing the playback speed, the DAW or sampler will eventually have to interpolate between these slices, since the necessary sound information is missing. Depending on the sampling rate, the sampler or the algorithm behind this process, this results in artefacts that can sound metallic, grainy or washed out.

You may need to repeat this step several times to get into this range depending on the DAW or sampler you are using. Ableton, for example, allows you to play an audio file up to eight times slower. If the result is still not extreme enough for you, you can render the file and repeat the process by slowing it down by a factor eight one more time. If your DAW or sampler offers different stretching algorithms, you should compare the different results and try going for variants that don't fit the sound you are processing. For Ableton, try 'beats' on pads, 'textures' on beats and so forth. I like to use 're-pitch' in the last step for percussion loops rich in overtones after I have already slowed down the loop several times with the 'textures' algorithm and am in the step of reducing the speed one last time from 16-times slower to 32-times slower. Just add in some reverb and delay and your ambient drone track is almost ready.

CLICKS & CUTZ

This last trick also works great in reverse. By playing loops or one-shots faster and faster, all that will remain is a noisy click. This is great for building interesting percussion and effect sounds. Although these sounds will end up being only a few milliseconds in length, they can be used to considerably enhance your drum racks if used cleverly and sparingly.

Alternatively, you can build click sounds by significantly reducing the decay, sustain and release settings of the original signal, a hi-hat for instance. In the second step, you program the midi notes. First, you have to zoom into the grid significantly.

In this example, I have set the grid to 1/256th. This means that I could now place 64 individual notes between each kick in a classic four-to-the-floor beat. At this playback speed, the brain can no longer distinguish between the individual instances of the hihat and perceives them as a single tonal or noisy unit, so be sure to check whether the tuning of the clicks matches the root note of your track. Changing the tempo or the spacing between your notes will change the pitch. You can also produce atonal clicks by programming less notes into the succession or by strongly varying the velocity values of the individual notes in your sequence.

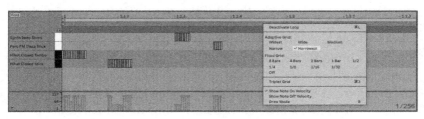

Image: Create new sounds by playing single notes in extremely quick succession.

Admittedly, this type of sound design is relatively time-consuming, but your effort will be rewarded with extraordinary and unique sounds.

WIDER SOUNDS WITH HARMONIZERS

Usually, pitch effects like harmonizers are mainly used to give voices more volume and width in the stereo image. But there's nothing stopping you from using this effect to fatten up other sounds as well. Harmonizers will usually let you control the frequency, timing (phase) and volume of the audio signal and are best suited for mono signals such as vocals or drums, but can also be effective for other instruments.

Harmonizers create several instances of the incoming signal and play them back with slight to strong shifts in timing and stereo panorama. In addition, harmonizers also use pitch-shifting to alter the pitch of the duplicated signals. Used subtly, this can add even more movement to your audio signal.

Through the panning settings and by applying a slight delay or detuning, you can now 'pull apart' the sound in the stereo panorama. If you increase the delay time or the frequency further, you will reach a point where the original and the duplicates are too far apart. From this point onwards, they will be perceived as separate sounds, which may also have its appeal.

If you've read this book carefully up to this point, you might have an alternate idea on how to simulate the harmonizer stereo effect. Basically, you can also do this by copying the signal to a second channel and panning both channels hard to the left and right of the stereo panorama. Now, you can pull one of the tracks back by a few milliseconds using track delay to create a similar effect. It's best to keep the track delay below 10 ms, since the brain will perceive the audio signals as a single unit up to this point. To round it off, you can also try to add pitch movement to the sound with the finetune setting or with the help of a pitch shifter plugin.

USING FILTERS AS OSCILLATORS

Did you know that you can use filters as a sound source? The technical term for this form of sound generation is self-oscillation and most resonant filters with a slope of at least 24 dB are capable of it.

To do this, you increase the resonance of the filter until it starts to whistle. In some cases, you may have to lower the edge of the frequency slowly using the cutoff. It may also be necessary to briefly ping the filter with noise to get this effect. But with most analog filters, it will happen by itself.

In the next step you tune the filter to your root note with the cutoff control. Now you have a clearly tuned sine wave coming out of your filter. Coupling the filter to the pitch (usually with keytrack = 100 percent) enables you to play it tonally - a perfect sound for sub basses or soft leads. If the filter also has control inputs (CV in), you can use these to control the pitch to achieve more kick-like sounds (envelope) or vibratos (LFO). In the next step, you can process the sound to your taste using the volume envelope.

BUILDING ATMOSPHERIC PADS WITH REVERB

You can create silky and smooth pads from audio signals sent through a reverb. All the tools you need to achieve this are a sampler, an EQ and a reverb. We start off with a tonal audio signal with as little modulation as possible and no audible peaks in volume. The underlying sample can be produced with a synth, a sampler or a field recorder.

First, you add an EQ to the insert effect chain of the channel housing the signal to rid it of low frequencies (cut everything under 200 Hz) and unnecessary resonance. Next, add the reverb plugin and set the dry/wet to 100 percent so that the only audible sound is the reverberated signal.

For sound design we will be using the parameters of the reverb effect. The reverb time (high decay values, large space settings, etc.) should be set to a high value. Reverb times of four to six seconds or longer are a good starting point. Our goal is to create a dense auditory fog from the original signal and the reverb. High values in the remaining parameters such as diffusion and feedback are also helpful.

If your reverb has a shimmer function, you can give the signal some extra brightness by introducing new harmonics. Afterwards, edit your sound with an EQ by removing unwanted frequencies that may have been introduced by the reverb.

Finally, render the channel as an audio file (freeze & bounce or resample). This way, you produce an audio snapshot of your diffuse sound cloud which will then be imported with the sampler of your choice.

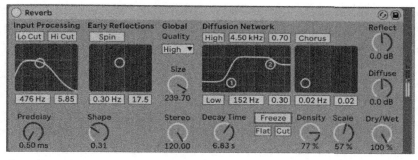

Tip: Experiment with the 'freeze' function for the best results (here: Ableton Reverb)

Now drag the audio file into the sampler. At this point, it will really pay off if you selected a non-modulated sound without prominent volume peaks. As you transpose the sound to higher octaves, its speed is increased and the attention is drawn to clicking, pronounced elements. This could be an interesting effect, but since we are going for silky pads here, it would just distract from what we want to achieve.

All that's left now is to work on the details in the sampler. Longer attack and release times on the amp envelope give the

pad a pleasant volume progression. After this, you can option-
ally introduce a modulated filter to make the sound more interesting. Panorama effects could also be interesting. Try off-
setting each voice slightly in the stereo image. Depending on
whether you started with a tonal or noisy base sound, you
should now correct the pitch - and that's it.

LAYERING PADS

It's no longer an insider tip to combine several pad sounds
with each other by layering them. Layering creates complex
soundscapes that don't get boring even over several bars. The
best approach is layering the pads across the frequency spectrum and/or distributed in the stereo panorama.

A midrange pad provides warmth and the basis for a more
modulated portion that occupies the upper midrange and high
frequencies. Afterwards, you feed both pads into a subtle
compressor and finally into an effects channel. This way, you
will apply reverb, delay and so forth to both parts equally and
acoustically glue them together.

Analog synth strings and acoustic string instruments work
together very well for this purpose. High-quality sample libraries offer a diverse range of styles - from delicate strum-
ming sounds to powerful ensembles. By layering acoustic
string sounds with your analog synth pads, you can infuse
your pads with an exciting touch and a distinct human feel.

AMBIENT SOUNDS WITH
DISTORTED REVERB

Overdrive, saturation and the like are known for adding dirt,
aggression or punch to an audio signal. By applying reverb,
they can also be used for powerful ambience.

For this trick, we want to roughen the reverb tail with a saturation plugin (alternatively, you can also use overdrive or distortion). This creates new harmonics that will translate into more shine and a vintage feeling.

For this, you drag a (shimmer-) reverb plugin into one of your effect sends and set the ratio to 100 percent wet. The next plugin in your effects chain will be an EQ, which will be used to optimally prepare the frequencies of the reverb tail for the subsequent saturation effect. Cut the low frequencies below 80 - 120 Hz and boost/cut the remaining spectrum to taste.

Since the overdrive plugin will react strongly to the level of the incoming signal, the EQ is an essential part of the sound design. Length (decay) and density (diffusion, density) of the reverb tail additionally affect the duration and intensity of the saturation. The most interesting results are achieved here by using pads for the reverb that develop high sonic dynamics over time through strong modulation.

CREATING HIHATS WITHOUT HIHATS

With this trick you can create hihats from any source audio with very little effort. All you need is a vocoder, ideally with at least eleven bands, a noise generator as a carrier, and a way to apply an envelope to the volume of the bands.

Such a vocoder is already included with the purchase of Ableton Live, users of other DAWs can download a free alternative in the TAL Vocoder for PC and MAC (https://tal-software.com/products/tal-vocoder).

First off, pick an audio channel that has distinct percussive character and clear transients. This will later form the basis for our hihats. If you want to keep the original channel in the mix without processing, you should duplicate it at this point and drag the vocoder into the new channel. Otherwise, you can just use the plugin's dry/wet control to determine the effect amount.

The vocoder is now ready for use. Our first step is to select a noise signal as the carrier. Either use the internal sound generation of the vocoder or feed an external noise source into it via the input. Set the effect level to at least 75 percent at the beginning so that you can clearly perceive changes in the sound. At this point, your input signal should already sound like a hihat.

Now, the actual sound design process begins. By using the frequency bands, you can lower certain frequencies or make them disappear completely. Vocoders can also be useful as filter banks from time to time. Ranging from subtle to radical, a vocoder will quickly give any signal a very special character. Tip: If your vocoder also has the ability to shift formants, you should definitely test this functionality on drum and percussion loops. Extreme shifts in particular can be a lot of fun.

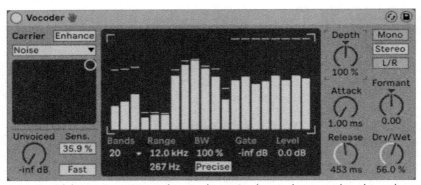

Image: Ableton Live Vocoder: It doesn't always have to be the robot voice. Vocoders are also a great tool for dynamic hihats.

The attack value determines how quickly the vocoder responds to volume changes in the input signal. Release will determine how long the filter bands hold the volume levels before they drop back to zero. Applying this to our example, longer release times will give you an open hihat, while shorter ones will produce a closed hihat. Very long release times are excellent in transitions. Slowly increase the release value in the break to gradually turn your closed hihat into a long, drawn-out noise.

SIMPLE HACKS FOR MORE EXCITING LEADS

The lead melody sounds good, but something still seems amiss? Try these two simple tricks.

METHOD 1 - THE COUNTERPART

This trick works especially well with melody progressions in which no more than two notes sound at the same time, i.e. with monophonic and duophonic synth leads. For this method, render your channel to audio and copy it to a new audio channel. Remember to lower the volume of both tracks a bit to balance the ratios in the mix.

Next, reverse one of the two melodies so that the file plays backwards and align the starting points of the first notes of both melodies. If you have used a relatively simple scale, both melodies should harmonize melodically. Don't worry if the distances between the notes of your melodies aren't exactly the same. If the notes overlap, this will result in chords with a note of unfamiliarity that is due to the reversed playback of one of your channels. Due to the similar frequency distribution in both tracks however, everything will fit together nicely.

If the lead melody becomes too dominant, delete individual parts of the reversed track to lighten the melodic load.

It is also possible to pan both tracks to the far right and left to clean up the mix a bit. If the melody plays for long periods of time in your track, try building up tension by occasionally deleting individual elements and automating the panning.

METHOD 2 - FLOATING TRANSITION

For this method, we start by creating a MIDI channel and dropping a software instrument or a hardware sound generator into it. The sound you choose here should be similar to the sound of your main melody in terms of character, but still independent enough to be clearly distinguishable. Copy the MIDI clip with the original main melody into the new track we have just created.

If your DAW allows it, I recommend zooming into both MIDI clips - the one in the main channel and the one in our copy - far enough so that you can comfortably see both melodies. Edit both melodies by selecting individual notes and deleting the corresponding note in the other channel.

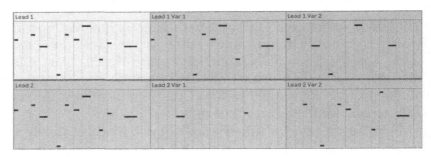

Image: On the left we have the original melody, in the middle an edit with a ratio of 80:20, on the right a variation including notes added later in the track.

For the ratio of the two channels to one another, you should start around 80:20 (main melody / counterpart). If your melody consisted of a total of ten notes at the beginning, you should see eight of them in the original channel and two of them in the counterpart channel after editing.

By progressively changing this ratio over time, you can create strong tonal variations with very little effort. Finally, you can add even more accents with a MIDI-synchronized delay on the counterpart channel by making both channels overlap slightly using delay repetitions.

COMBINING ARPEGGIATORS

Arpeggiators are a great tool for electronic music production. They can be used to create complex rhythms and melodies with very little effort. If your DAW is equipped to do so, experiment with combining several arpeggiators in a sequence and test different gate lengths, octaves and speeds.

In general, and especially in a sequence, it's worthwhile setting at least one of them to 'random', as this often results in completely new melody progressions. By recording the audio or MIDI output of your channel, you can preserve this randomized material for eternity.

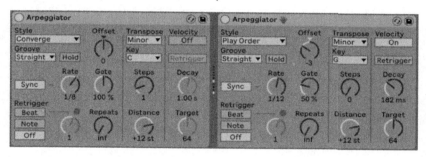

Image: Using two arpeggiators in sequence, triplet patterns are applied to an 8th note beat. By applying a 16th note swing in the second arpeggiator we also add an additional shuffle feeling.

You can also try applying arpeggiators to percussion and drum tracks. This allows you to create complex drum patterns without programming knowledge - a perfect tool for experimental genres such as ambient or IDM. If you like extremes, you can also vary the speeds of the individual arpeggiators via automation.

CREATIVE GATING EFFECTS WITH TREMOLO

We have already discussed the use of tremolo and auto pan plugins as duckers. Now we will look at how to create complex gating effects using these plugins to produce rhythmically chopped pads with surprisingly little effort.

If you are using a DAW other than Ableton, you can recreate this trick with the freeware Pecheng Tremolo. You can find VST and AU versions here: http://pechenegfx.blogspot.com/2014/11/the-plugin-pecheneg-tremolo.html.

First off, we load three instances of the auto pan plugin into our channel in sequence as an insert. As we did with ducking, we now remove the stereo effect from all instances by adjusting the phase of the LFOs and setting it to 0° (or 360°).

Next, we select an oscillation mode for the volume reduction of the gate effect. Anything will work here, but to achieve a controlled effect I would avoid the random setting for now. For our example, I selected sine once and sawtooth twice. By clicking on the note symbol, I can synchronize the LFOs to the beat of my track.

Image: Several tremolos in sequence are great for creative gating effects.

The 'rate' parameter determines the speed of the individual gate effects. This is where our trick comes into play: by choosing different speeds for every LFO, we can create a complex rhythmic chopping effect that is applied to our audio signal. Because we have locked the speeds to our track with the note signal, these rhythms will always run in sync with our beat. Combinations of even and triplet beats, such as 1/4th, 1/6th and 1/16th work especially well here.

Using offset and shape, we can now finetune our gating effect and determine, if the effect should be very defined or more soft and whether the rhythm should shuffle 'forward' or be more 'laid back'. By slightly increasing the phase control of one of the LFOs, you can add some stereo width to the signal.

POLYRHYTHMIC LOOPS

Historically, polyrhythmic structures are relatively new in western music. In polyrhythms, two or more different rhythms overlap simultaneously, and each channel may have its own beat. Especially in electronic music, which can be very repetitive, rigid patterns can suddenly be filled with new life. For our example, I will apply this concept to drum sounds, but you may want to try polyrhythms on bass or synth channels as well.

Let's start off with a beat with 4/4 timing and set the kick to 1, 2, 3 and 4. In a second channel, we create a MIDI clip for our percussion sound. Set the grid in the empty MIDI clip to triplets (triplet grid or 3t division), dividing the clip into 24 steps instead of 16. Insert notes at equal intervals against the kick (see image). You can slightly emphasize the first beat of the triplet pattern by raising the volume (velocity).

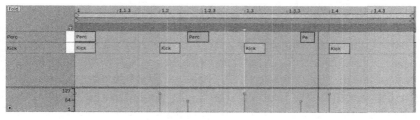

Image: Kick and percussion patterns

If you listen to both channels together, you should now be able to clearly count 1-2-3-4, 1-2-3-4 on the kick and 1-2-3, 1-2-3 on the percussion sound. The length of the clip will determine the point at which the pattern repeats. If you loop both clips, they will coincide sooner or later.

For really complex beats, you can add more sequences set to different time signatures that play against the 4/4 kick. In this example, I used a hi-hat sample, places a note on 1 and looped the clip after five steps.

A slightly different but no less exciting approach is to cut samples roughly so they don't loop to the grid. If a sample would end after four bars, you can simply cut a bit off at the end, making it repeat after bar 3.2.3, for example. The kick should continue to set the rigid 4/4 pattern so the track won't get too chaotic. The kick sets an auditory anchor to make sure our individual tracks don't derail it. Effects and atmospheric sounds are also great candidates for uneven loops.

BACKGROUND ATMOSPHERES TO TIE THE TRACK TOGETHER

Many producers use this simple trick to give their tracks a subtle framework that ties all elements together and makes the track seem fuller overall. Used the right way, background atmospheres can work wonders.

You can use anything from noise over field recordings to reverb-laden synth pads. The important thing is to cut out all superfluous high and low frequencies, and to make sure that the signal works very subtly in the background only. I'm a big fan of field recordings, such as the sound of an airport terminal or a summer meadow. By introducing constant movement in the very background of the track, you introduce variations that you might not be able to hear directly, but that have a big influence on the feel of the track.

___ CLOSING REMARKS...

We have reached the end of the book 'Producing Electronic Music'. First of all, I am very glad you made it this far. Hopefully, many of the tips described have inspired you and help you with your production.

Thanks again for choosing this book. I would be very happy to read your review on Amazon.

Feel free to share what you have learned with friends and help them improve as well. If you have enjoyed this book and think it would also help your friends out, I would be ecstatic about a recommendation.

Hamburg, May 2021